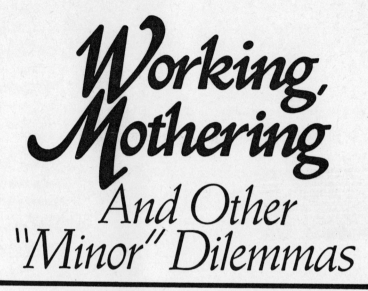

Working, Mothering

And Other "Minor" Dilemmas

AN INSPIRATIONAL GUIDEBOOK FOR RAISING KIDS WHILE WORKING IN AND OUT OF THE HOME

Melodie M. Davis

WORD BOOKS
PUBLISHER
WACO, TEXAS
A DIVISION OF
WORD, INCORPORATED

Scripture quotations are from the *Holy Bible: New International
Version.* Copyright © 1978 by the New York International Bible
Society. Used by permission of Zondervan Bible Publishers.

Library of Congress Cataloging in Publication Data

Davis, Melodie M., 1951–
   Working, mothering, and other "minor" dilemmas.

   1. Mothers—Psychology. 2. Mothers—Employment—
Psychological aspects. 3. Children—Religious life.
4. Parenting. 5. Child development. 6. Family. I. Title.
HQ759.D29 1984   649'.1   84-7483
ISBN 0-8499-0375-0

Printed in the United States of America

To my daughters,
Michelle and Tanya

Contents

9

Contents

Preface

I grew up during the fifties and sixties when young girls received a lot of advice (implicit and explicit) on how to be a wife and mother. Role models were all around me: my mom, aunts, neighbors, women at church—wonderful, dedicated, accomplished women who, for the most part, found satisfaction and fulfillment in caring for their homes and families.

Then I did some more growing up in the seventies when I received *more* advice—on how to have a career. In society there were all kinds of "new" role models: lawyers, doctors, merchants, chiefs. Superwomen! It was exciting, and along with many others, I postponed motherhood in pursuit of a paycheck.

Now there's a new breed of mothers trying to bring it all together. Mostly we've given up trying to be *super*women— our jobs aren't so glamorous and our homes not so posh. And for those of us who happen to be committed to Christ as well, there aren't many role models or manuals written from a Christian perspective that help with the practical nuts and bolts of raising kids while holding a job.

Not that being a mother today is all that different from what it was in my mother's generation. There are still kids to chauffeur, childhood illnesses to get through, diapers to change, and joyful moments of pure gold when the toddler first bows her head and jabbers a copycat prayer.

But mothers twenty, even ten years ago didn't talk much about if and when to have kids, whether to take natural childbirth classes, how to involve father, how to find good child care, what to do when the kids are sick and you can't miss work. In many ways, being a mother in the eighties and beyond is a new day in parenting. There are new questions: Does postponing parenthood increase the risk of infertility? What effect do increased additives in diets have on the occurrence of hyperactivity in children? How can traditionally family-oriented times like Christmas and summer still be meaningful on a slimmed-down budget of time and money? Coping with transitions into and out of paid employment, taking time to be "children" ourselves, helping TV foster family togetherness instead of alienation . . . these are some of the things that make parenting different now.

I am not Dr. Spock or Dr. Dobson. I am not even very far along in my journey as wife, mother, and employee. But if I'm lacking in expertise, I'm up to my ears (and sometimes over my head) in experience—the experience of keeping a toddler happy while trying to cook supper and relax after work, of vaccinations and infant stimulation and scheduling coordinated vacations. And while I have a variety of friends and acquaintances including singles, divorcees, child-free couples, full-time homemakers, I'm also very much aware that I'm surrounded by a whole bevy of women more or less like me—in their late twenties or thirties, with a youngster or two in tow or one hatching, working part- or full-time outside the home (or planning to work), while still trying to keep up with things like summer canning or winter needlework and still allow time for husband, for self, and for God. Many of us wish we could be home full-time, but feel we have no choice

12

if we want to live even in a modest home with adequate clothes and food. Others of us are glad to get out of the house two or more days a week and do something besides wipe runny noses.

But beyond the nuts-and-bolts issues of what to do for a stubborn first grader or a bad case of colic, I hope this book gives perspectives on how each child is a gift from God who helps us mature, be patient, and learn how to laugh and smile more deeply than we have before!

Acknowledgments

Like most writers, I'm aware that many people have influenced the writing of this book; I have simply put the words on paper. I'm indebted first of all to my family at this point in life—Stuart, Michelle, and Tanya, who was born after this manuscript was completed; to the family I grew up in—Mom, Dad, Nancy, Linda, and Terry from whom I've drawn for countless illustrations; to my work family—Evelyn Sauder, typist and confidante; Pam Beverage, Ron Byler, Lowell Hertzler, Ken Weaver, and Paul Yoder, encouragers; Margaret Foth, who originally used most of these chapters on her "Your Time" radio program; to my extended family in Virginia and elsewhere; to my publishing "family" at Word Books for believing this was a book "whose time had come"; and finally to Linda Payne and family, who through providing a loving home for Michelle and Tanya enable me to feel good about "working and mothering."

1

Won't Somebody
Give Me a Job Description?

When I was attempting to get my office in order before
beginning a three-month maternity leave, I wrote a detailed
task list of items complete with deadlines. Mostly as a joke, I
scrawled two final items on my list: "Have baby April 22."
"Return to work July 7."

Michelle Dawn squeaked in just seventeen minutes past
her deadline. Not bad, even in a writer's world of rigid deadlines. I thought this mothering thing would be a breeze.

I had requested that my baby "room in" with me at the
hospital, which meant that I had all responsibility for her from
baths to diapers to cuddling. But that breezy high from giving
birth drifted right out the window when I tried to change her
first diaper. I had used up fifteen cotton balls and a vial of
sterile water and she still wasn't clean. "Do I have to clean up
every little bit?" I asked the stern-looking nurse who answered my push on the panic button. By the way she looked
at me, I immediately realized that my question was as dumb
to her as asking a plumber if just a little leak wouldn't be okay.
I envisioned every diaper change taking fifteen minutes and
wondered how I'd ever manage it all.

15

Three months of full-time mothering was luxury. Oh, I was tired and slept a lot and worked even more, but gradually I regained all the composure I had lost under that nurse's stare. However, as my deadline to return to the office part-time approached, I began to wonder how I would ever handle everything plus twenty hours a week away from home. What would I do when Michelle was sick? How could I give full energy to a job if she got us up three times in the night? What would I do if the babysitter called in the middle of a high-level business meeting?

And then I remembered that although my boss and I had outlined a careful job description for my work at the office, nobody had thought to give me one for the so-called "working mom." (A misnomer because *all* moms work; why don't we call employed fathers "working dads"?)

Now I know there's no job description because it would be so long and so diverse that no woman would have time to read it, much less worry about it. But I did need some directives for doing the delicate balancing act of being a mother and holding a job, too. I was torn. At home I enjoyed my daughter, but felt I was falling behind at the office. At the office I enjoyed my work, but chastised myself for falling behind in my housework, my parenting, my marriage, and my personal life. I felt guilty for leaving Michelle during the day, and guilty that when I got home from work sometimes all I felt like doing was reading the paper. ("Quality" time? 4:30 P.M. is not my best time of day, nor is it for most infants I know.) Yet the magazines intended for helping working moms cope talked of hired housekeepers and other unheard-of luxuries, and seemed so empty from my viewpoint as a Christian.

Then someone gave me a stress test—one of those score-it-yourself questionnaires where you fill in blanks and then look up the results in an answer key. I flunked. My score was so terrible it registered off the bottom end of the answer table.

Because I was so *happy,* it hadn't really occurred to me that I was going through a particularly stressful period of life. My days, though hectic, were brimming with love, laughter, and the contentment of nursing a cuddly little mophead. But in the course of a year I had experienced pregnancy; the addition of a new family member; business readjustment; change in financial state; change to a different line of work; change in responsibilities at work; change in living conditions, work hours, sleeping and eating habits, social activities, and more . . . enough to make me a candidate for a nervous breakdown.

That stress test helped me recognize that all my doubts and feelings of disorientation were normal reactions to a stressful situation. When I became uptight about baby paraphernalia spread over the living room, I did one of the relaxation exercises learned in Lamaze class and told myself, "Ah ha—let's see, the stress test called this 'change in living conditions.'" I knew this drastic shift in roles was going to take some time to get used to.

A role change can affect the basic way in which we look at ourselves. It's like looking at a different person inside the same old body. That can be disorienting.

For instance, when I first announced my pregnancy and desire to return to work half-time, I began to feel like I was just treading water—keeping busy, but not getting anywhere. It seemed that my colleagues started to confer more with each other on business than with me. At times there were meetings I didn't need to attend because they related to items that would be occurring during my leave of absence. And I began to wonder if the others resented the need to pick up my work while I was on leave, and whether down deep they thought a maternity leave was an unfair benefit.

One night I told my husband, "Help! I'm having an identity crisis!" But I was determined not to pity myself or succumb to feelings of "nobody needs me." Together my husband

and I talked about a series of incidents that had made me feel left out, and I was able to better understand what was happening.

I think the first step in coping with stress brought on by a role change is to own up to the fact the change *is* occurring. Saying that "nothing will be changed by my working half-time" is not dealing with reality. I had to recognize that the job definitions of others had shifted also, since someone else would be doing the work I formerly covered. So it wasn't that they were trying to take away my authority; they were just filling new and different roles, too.

Next, I needed to welcome the fact that change was occurring. I'd wanted to see some changes in my job anyway.

The third step was to continue to assert myself when I felt left out. I think an attitude of "they don't consult me anymore" makes a person look at everyone else suspiciously, and this only tends to drive others away. Also, I think it's probably true that a "nobody needs me" attitude makes a person *become* less creative and therefore less needed. On the other hand, if we assume our ideas are still welcome and sought after, we tend to remain on the creative, growing edge.

In any role change, it may take a period of months or even years to work out a comfortable, new identity. One young mother said, "It took me three years to feel comfortable about being a mother. Now it's starting to be fun. But if you don't have yourself squared away, if you haven't worked out your own identity and values, it's practically impossible to be a mother."[1]

My husband and I also had to find new ways of relating to each other, not only to the baby. One man said, "Once you have a baby, you might as well kiss each other goodbye and say, 'So long. I'll see you in twenty years.'"

Well, I wouldn't go that far, but our relationship as a couple did change. I remember one Saturday morning when my sister and her husband surprised me at 8:30 A.M. with a leisurely long-distance call. (They don't have any kids.) She was still in their waterbed, they were going out for breakfast, and just called to chat. I turned a little green, remembering the nice years of an occasional Saturday breakfast out. Now it seemed more hassle than it was worth. (To be fair to my sister and other child-free couples, that morning was a luxury for her also. Saturdays usually find her out coaching a basketball team or leading a wilderness camping expedition.)

Instead of being alone whenever we want to be, my husband and I have to plan times for intimacy, especially since we both work outside the home. This can spoil spontaneity and sharing. So it's good to *try* to save at least a brief period each day to be alone together.

New roles also require a different way of dividing up household chores. This is a highly individual matter because what works in one family might not work in another. Sheila shared how going to work after her three children were in school affected their household chores. "I've found out the world doesn't fall apart if the oven doesn't get cleaned, and Bill's learned it's a drag to get down and wash the kitchen floor and wax it and then have someone come and walk their dirty boots over it. He didn't know that before. He couldn't figure out why I'd suddenly lose my mind when someone dirtied up my clean floor."[2] If both partners agree to the importance of having a second income, then it will be easier to resolve the issue of who does what at home.

Usually role changes of any kind also involve a change in the amount of money coming into a home. This can be a potential source of conflict, whether it means more income than before, or less. But having less may not be all bad.

At least one couple I know who went from two paychecks to one said, "We don't really miss the second paycheck. We're spending less on fast food, we don't have the babysitting to pay for, and we find we need fewer dress-up clothes." So, chances are, after some initial worries over how to manage with a change in income, things will work themselves out. We just stop spending when the bank account is empty!

I've found it's helpful to talk about a change in income with others who've gone through the same thing. It seems that financial problems are the last taboo in terms of what we're willing to share with outsiders. If you find it difficult to talk about financial problems with friends, perhaps a less involved third party would be more helpful. Consider consulting a financial counselor, a pastor, or a marriage counselor for help.

I feel that God cares about helping us find answers even to our earthly problems like finances. But it will take some real human effort to understand conflicts over money and how role changes sometimes affect a marriage in regard to money issues.

Having new roles means we will make mistakes. Probably nothing is as demeaning or frustrating as having an overly anxious grandmother or neighbor tell us how the baby should be clothed, fed, or disciplined. But it's important to allow ourselves a margin for mistakes because then the triumphs are also our own—like our discovery that at first we were dressing Michelle too warmly.

People who have studied the transition to parenthood say that the possibility for crisis exists for three main reasons. The first is that *parenthood arrives abruptly.* Although there are nine long months of actual preparation and perhaps several years of "just thinking about" parenthood, the switch to parenthood comes overnight—we arrived at the hospital a twosome and went home a threesome. Sociologists say that a group of two people is the most stable human grouping, while a three-person group is the most volatile.[3]

The second reason becoming a parent is so traumatic is that *parenthood is the only major life role for which there is no preparation.* As the saying goes, "It's the only course in which you get your degree first and then have to do all the course work afterward." Some new mothers and fathers think that their earlier babysitting experiences or occasional contact with nieces and nephews have prepared them adequately for a baby. But it's different to be responsible for a young life twenty-four hours a day.

The last reason the switch to parenthood can be so jolting is that *it is irrevocable!* There are no refunds or exchanges. This reality staring new parents in the face can be frightening.

After saying all this, it's encouraging and uplifting to see the scores of young parents who do eventually adjust to their new roles. Our friends Tim and Karen said it this way: "We just can't imagine what life would be like without Shawn, Rachel, and Wesley. We wouldn't have it any other way."

Isn't it amazing that the human body and mind stand up as well as they do under constant change? Time has a way of helping us along. God has created us with the ability to heal, and to adjust to what at first seem like difficult situations.

2

Who'll Change the Diaper
in the Middle of the Night?

Knowing that the transition to parenthood is usually stressful, many couples today (and we were one of them) debate long and loud: "Should we have a baby?" Along with a whole generation of men and women, we deliberately postponed having a family. We went out to dinner without worrying about getting a babysitter, slept in on Saturday morning without kids storming the bedroom, and used our earnings for things other than Pampers, potty chairs, and Pablum!

Suddenly I was twenty-six and found myself watching mothers and kids in supermarkets enviously. Should we have children? Should I quit work for three months, six months, a year, five years? What will happen to my career in the meantime? Could I manage part-time work with a family? What about day care? The decisions were not easy, and neither is living with them afterwards!

Why did we want to have a child? Human beings may be able to design computers modeled on the human brain, but most of us can't really answer that question.

The choices are certainly different than they used to be,

aren't they? Although Mom and Dad had certain choices as to birth control, lifestyle, and so on, our folks hardly even considered whether or not they would have children. It was the expected, normal pattern. A couple got married and then, as sure as dirty dishes and income tax, they had a baby . . . or three or four.

Now, however, we worry about things as frivolous as who'll change the diaper in the middle of the night and as heavy as why have kids in a world threatened by nuclear holocaust.

An editorial in *Family Life* magazine says that we have challenged the myths of parenting in this decade;[1] we no longer believe that children will provide marital happiness and cement a couple together. Many of us are well aware that having children involves physical risks, a heavy cash investment, an equally heavy emotional investment, and sacrifices in personal freedom, with no guarantees that the child will not turn out to be a thief, a drug addict, or an alcoholic.

Then why do couples today make the decision to take what Margaret Marius in the journal, *Family Coordinator,* calls "perhaps . . . the biggest gamble of a lifetime"?[2] Some women and men feel they need to have a child to be completely "man" or "woman." Others give in to pressure from *their* parents. Couples may have children so they'll have someone to take care of them when they're older, to have a feeling of being loved and needed.[3] Some may just enjoy loving and being with children; others find a challenge in bringing up children who will contribute to society, God's kingdom, and the future.

We may have subconscious desires to live out unfulfilled dreams and hopes through a new generation. We think of sharing in creativity, of gaining a kind of immortality through our children. As Malcolm Muggeridge said, "They give you a tremendous sense of the glory of life."[4]

When I think about how much richer my life is because I'm

fortunate enough to have children—how much I have learned and grown—then even diapers and teething seem worth it. Of course, this growth is also possible in other ways, but lately I have become very much aware of how tenderly children nourish adults. Our pastor says that when he must be away from his wife and small son for several days—away from their love and caring touch—he just doesn't feel as "together" or as well emotionally.

This is not to say that every couple *should* choose to have children. The statistics on abused and battered children show clearly that not all adults make good parents. Also, some people have careers or involvements which demand too much time and emotional energy. The sister I mentioned earlier is a physical education teacher and coach. She must spend many hours with the athletic teams outside of school hours. Through this close contact she has been able to relate to many young women. Instead of being a parent to one, two, or three children, she is a substitute parent and friend for many kids at times in their lives when some are having difficulty relating to their real parents. I think we need to respect and accept others in the decisions they make regarding having families. It is, after all, a very personal decision.

One of the biggest questions many couples face when it comes to deciding whether to have children is the issue of jobs and careers. Increasingly, the family making this decision is a family in which both husband and wife hold full-time jobs outside the home. And it's the wife who usually struggles with whether to quit or curtail her outside work to take up the primary tasks of nurturing an infant. Although I know of several delightful couples who have decided the husband will stay home to take care of a young child, this is still the exception to the rule.

The ideal arrangement, of course, is one in which parenthood can be equally shared by fathers and mothers. But this would take changes in society that probably won't take place

24

for quite awhile. It takes a flexible job situation that allows each to work part-time or unusual hours. And this is not possible for many people at the present time.

Probably one of the reasons women fear leaving the job world to take up baby feedings and baths is that they've heard "horror stories" from other young mothers—accounts of days alone with no one over two years old to talk to, or of realizing that out of habit they have reached over at a dinner party and cut their neighbor's meat into bite-sized pieces. Others fear that staying home with a new baby will cause them to "dry up," to lose touch with the rapid changes in their fields or destroy their chances of advancing in their careers. Or, if they decide to combine motherhood and career, they are afraid having a baby will mean having less creative energy to put into their job.

I think such fears are natural—and, to a certain extent, well founded. But there's another side to the issue. One young mother, Nancy McGrath, wrote about her one-year-old daughter, Sarah. "Since I left work to become her mother, I've lost professional momentum . . . and I know that when I go hunting for another job I may feel that loss sharply. But in the meantime, Sarah has made such a *present* of her eagerness, her quick sense of humor, her cockeyed, pell-mell walk, her crooked grin and, lately, her almost boundless affection, that I'm sure I haven't lost out on the deal."[5] To describe Sarah's "almost boundless affection," Sarah's father writes, "Sarah is having a love affair with the world. . . . She kisses not only Nancy and me and her yellow dog, but her crib and the high chair and the front door! . . . I can watch her for hours."[6]

The sacrifice of losing out in a job for a few months or years is compensated by the sheer joy of watching a child grow.

While some prospective parents naïvely perceive having babies as all love, coos, wet kisses, and pretty, soft skin, others focus too heavily on the negatives. And while I think it's important for a couple to be realistic, to be aware of some possible difficult experiences in having children, I don't think we should focus too heavily on them or become too burdened by the possibilities. All living requires faith. And God promises strength as we need it. The hard times bring growth. But generally the frightening and the difficult are overshadowed by the bright sunshine a child can bring into the home.

It's helpful for the young mother to know that the husband may experience a bit of jealousy when the new baby arrives. Formerly, he didn't need to share his wife's affection, time, and attention with anyone! Now there's a little boy or girl who seems to demand these from both husband and wife. Exhaustion—and sometimes depression—sets in with the irregular schedule of newborn care. Such changes in lifestyle naturally demand understanding, a willingness to cope with whatever comes along, and a generous helping of "sense of humor." I think it is very important that mother *and* father work at parenting. Unless fathers make a special effort, they lose out on the joys of feeling the growing responsiveness of a baby, of sharing the accomplishment and discovery of the toddler—of building a relationship!

Having a baby brings new insight about ourselves and our relationship to each other. We'll understand in new ways our own mothers or fathers and how they brought us up. We'll marvel at God's infinite skill, ability, and wisdom in the birth process. Through our children, we change and grow in ways that mellow and equip us for all of life's experiences.

And we *can* stay alive intellectually—keep on growing personally. We can fill spare moments with good books and magazines and keep in contact with friends who stimulate thinking. The church offers friendships and fellowship groups through which we can expand our horizons.

Parents the world around agree that children are truly a gift from God. We may not *always* feel that way, of course, but in precious moments we see it in fresh ways: when the pre-schooler pats a sobbing pal soothing, "There, there"; when the grade-schooler brings home a poem dedicated to "My Mother"; when the toddler sits down and crosses his legs exactly like his father does.

God has marvelously outfitted us with the skills and patience to cope with the changes and the new choices we have in present society. We not only can survive the challenges of raising children, but we can blossom and mature through them.

3

A Funny Thing
Happened on Our Way to Parenthood

Dr. Bump looked so serious and clinical in his crisp white coat. "There's one thing I want you to consider very carefully," he said solemnly, "before we start giving you a bunch of tests for infertility."

I winced at that word, not wanting to apply it to myself.

"You need to resolve in your own mind how badly you want a child. Treating infertility can be very expensive and the tests very painful. Have you and your husband talked about how far you want to go with the testing?"

No, we really hadn't discussed the cost, or to what lengths we would go. But as I thought about the up-and-down emotions of the last two and a half years as we tried to conceive a child, and about the envy I felt toward the rounded mothers-to-be sitting that very moment in his waiting room, and about the ache inside me lately when I was around tiny babies, I didn't hesitate much with an answer.

"Yes, I think we're ready to go through with whatever testing you recommend," I said.

He shook my hand and sent me out to the nurse, who

explained how to keep a temperature chart for the first month.

And then a funny thing happened on our way to parenthood. Little did we know, but I was already two weeks pregnant at the time. In about a month I was back to see him, suspecting pregnancy.

"Cured already, huh?" he joked as he began a routine prenatal examination.

For those who have gone through two, five, ten, or even fifteen years of testing and waiting to have a baby, my quick "fix" must seem like a cruel hoax. There is no way that I can pretend to identify with those whose ordeals with infertility have been excruciating and extended. But my short experience did sensitize me to some of the emotions and issues involved in infertility.

I talked to one woman who tried for years to have a baby. I'll call her Leanna. She said she thinks that because women today assume they have choices about career and motherhood, it's a real blow all of a sudden *not* to be in control. As she put it, "You *think* you have this choice about motherhood and so you choose it, and then nothing happens!"

Experts estimate today that about 15 percent of all couples have some difficulty in conceiving a child.[1] That number seems to have risen in recent years. Possibly this is because more and more couples are postponing parenthood to less fertile years. Or perhaps it is just that people are more open about discussing their conception difficulties and consulting a doctor about treatments.

I am not a doctor, and it would be presumptuous for me to try to describe all the various causes of infertility or treatments. They're often complicated, and it's best to get that kind of information straight from an expert. But I do know that the feelings and attitudes associated with infertility can be as much of a problem as the physical side.

Leanna said that seeing other parents mistreat their children was extremely difficult for her to tolerate. She said, "I just want to say to them, 'Oh, you don't know how you should *treasure* that child.'"

On a different note, Leanna commented that it was also hard for her to be around obviously happy families. "You want what they have so much, yet you can't have it," she related. "Going to baby showers, seeing pregnant women, watching mothers with their babies can all cause a lump in the throat or bring on a spell of bitterness."

She also said she noticed that so many TV ads picture happy babies and young children. Now, there's nothing wrong with that, but for her it was one more painful reminder of what was missing in her life.

Leanna went on to tell me how she and her husband had purposely postponed having a family. First, they worked their way through graduate school together. Then she taught college classes while her husband completed a doctorate.

Finally, Leanna and Tom decided it was time to start their family. They moved to a new town, and Leanna didn't bother to get a job teaching, since they thought she would soon be pregnant. She said, "After about a year of trying, you start wondering—is there something wrong?" They began seeing a doctor, who recommended *against* extensive, complicated tests because in his experience many of the more complicated tests were not conclusive.

They did go through a number of the more routine tests, which was discouraging because in their case nothing seemed to be "wrong." All the tests came out all right, and this was even more difficult to face. "You don't know what you're dealing with. The doctors said they didn't really know why we were having trouble conceiving," Leanna said.

Leanna and Tom feel they were drawn closer by their experience of dealing with infertility, even though the various tests, charts, and scheduling of intercourse often can rob a couple of intimacy. The unique rapport they shared had always made them exceptionally close as a couple. So Leanna found talking things over with her husband to be a real source of strength. They grew in their love. She says, "A woman shouldn't carry the burden herself. If it's difficult for your husband to talk about infertility, you need *someone* in whom you can confide, or the struggle will be overwhelmingly lonely."

What else helped her and Tom keep going during the difficult years? Leanna eventually went back to work to get her mind off herself, and she felt much better. She said that although she had always been very healthy, while she was not working and was trying to conceive she had felt worse physically than she ever had in her life.

Other couples coping with infertility have taken in foster children, or become involved with programs like Big Brothers-Big Sisters, to help them fulfill their desire to have children in their lives.

I've known some couples who say that their faith in God's will for their lives was a real source of strength in coping with infertility, but God deals with each of us individually. Strangely, Leanna says, although she knew God loved her and Tom, her faith in God wasn't necessarily helpful during this time. She continued believing, but it wasn't as if God was an easy answer to their problem.

Despite the difficulties, there's a happy ending to their story. Leanna and Tom applied for an adoption, and after one and a half years, they received a call while they were vacationing out of state one Christmas.

"Do you still want a child?" the voice on the other end of the line asked.

"We sure do." They hurried home, picking up their six-week-old son on the way! The following August, Leanna found she was pregnant, so now they're the happy, dedicated parents of two charming boys. She says, "Each child was a gift, in a different way."

The outcome was different for another woman, Eileen. She decided that pursuing a battery of tests could destroy her relationship with the only real family she had, her husband. What if they discovered whose "fault" the infertility was? In addition to feeling left out of parenthood, the one responsible would probably suffer a lot of guilt, too.

She said, "I finally realized my husband and I together were a pretty fine family. We had believed this seven years earlier when we married, and with the help of . . . love . . . the two of us would continue to grow as a family."[2]

I think what infertility does say is that children are indeed gifts from God. So that makes any child a new witness to the miracle of creation! That may be hard to remember when Billy has just asked for the hundredth time why caterpillars are fuzzy—but he's a miracle nevertheless. When I think of all the circumstances that have to be just right for conception to take place, it becomes an even greater miracle. One infertility specialist says that a healthy woman who is exposed to active sperm at the precise time of ovulation has only a 10 percent chance of becoming pregnant.[3]

So if we have children, we can be grateful. I know it's tough some days to be a parent, and some persons don't have the resources for coping. But I think most parents get to the place where they realize they didn't appreciate their children as much as they could have during the growing up years.

We can also be more understanding, sympathetic, and less nosy towards those who can't or don't have children. While children are a gift from God, they're not the only gift fulfilling man and woman. Commitment to a fulfilling job or mission are also possibilities.

The key is to go on living our lives as fully as possible, regardless of circumstances. Don't postpone living waiting for a baby, or for a master's degree, or for a mate, or for that next promotion. These aren't the things that bring lasting happiness. Rather, happiness comes from peace with God, peace with ourselves, and peace with our neighbors.

4

I Can Hardly Wait
to Get into Maternity Clothes

"You mean that's it?" I asked the doctor as he nonchalantly finished examining me and told me to get dressed. "You mean I'm pregnant and you're not even going to give me one of those rabbit tests?"

He smiled faintly. "No, with the home test that you did and the fact that your uterus has already started enlarging, I can positively confirm your pregnancy."

He was so calm. I was swirling. He was so doctorly and professional. I was in awe and deliriously happy. To him it was just a routine pregnancy. To me life would never be the same.

Back at the office, I struggled to keep my mind on boring reports and memos. How long should I wait to tell my boss? What would he do about my request to work half-time? Would the company be able to grant the three-month maternity leave I thought I wanted?

The employed woman not only gets the fun of telling family and friends about the expected baby, but struggles with how to talk about it appropriately at work. I squelched the desire to post a big announcement on the bulletin board or to shock everyone at a staff meeting. I didn't dash off a memo or proclaim it on the intercom.

Beyond telling my immediate supervisors and a few close friends at the office, mostly I decided to wait and let the gentler media of maternity clothes get my message across. (Of course, I couldn't wait to get into those billowy dresses and tops—not knowing how long nine months would get!)

Expecting a child is a very special time of introspection. Feeling depressed during pregnancy is common. I kept getting bigger and clumsier—and just wanted the baby to hurry up and come. I found that being physically able to continue working did help to keep my mind off myself. Unfortunately, some women become too ill or face hazardous conditions on the job, making work impossible.

I know there were times at work when I simply wished everyone would forget I was pregnant. I got so tired of questions like when are you due, how are you feeling, do you want a boy or girl? Of course, I was glad people were interested, but it began to feel as though I was no longer valued for myself alone.

There were other times I felt the meetings and briefings and reports were irrelevant compared to the miracle of the growing baby inside me.

But even as I withdrew into myself, I realized that it was terribly refreshing and important to simply force myself to talk about something other than babies. At mealtime, I tried to think actively of things other than pregnancy to chat about with my husband. (Or at least I tried after a tactful reminder one day that sometimes he got tired of hearing about nausea, backache, and what the doctor said!) I also tried not to bore my co-workers with a running report on the state of my swollen ankles.

It's one thing to prepare the layette and nursery in anticipation of the baby's arrival, but preparing yourself emotionally is a much more difficult and important task. How do you get ready to be a parent?

Well, as one young mother so aptly put it, "You don't. If you wait until you think you're ready to have children, you'll never have them."

Connie put it this way, "I've always said God planned for babies to enter our lives a little at a time. At first they sleep practically all the time. Then, little by little, they demand more and more of your time." (She must have had a quiet baby who didn't have colic the first three months!)

One way to prepare is by comparing notes with other expectant parents. Even though I didn't live near enough to a sorority of aunts and sisters to benefit(?) from the "traditional" prenatal horror tales, I did find a good friend who could empathize with my feelings, doubts, and joys.

The marvelous thing about pregnancy is that most of the process is automatic, like a built-in baby machine. Nature takes care to see that the baby is protected by a cushion of fluid that shields the baby from accidental knocks and bruises. The uterus grows and the other organs get squished closer together for a time, all without so much as a moment's thought on the part of the mother. Even the emotional highs and lows somehow even out, so that most women can keep their jobs and keep up an active social and physical life. Pregnancy is not a disease, and fortunately, physicians are no longer treating it as such.

While pregnancy is a normal condition, the growing baby does make increasing demands on the mother's body. Most pregnant women find they are more tired than usual. I have the luxury of a private office, and I found that just lying down on the floor for fifteen minutes at coffee break gave me new energy for my work. In a factory, hospital, or restaurant, it may be more difficult to find a quiet place to rest, but expectant mothers needn't be shy about staking out the lounge sofa as "theirs" for a few restful minutes.

In a second or third pregnancy, parents agonize over how the new little one will be accepted. For a three-year-old, the concept of an unborn baby can be totally otherworldly. How can a baby breathe inside the "tummy"? How did it get there?

Answering the many questions as simply and lovingly as possible helps in the adjustment. One three-year-old, upon learning that Mommy was going to have a baby, wanted the baby to *get out now*. Nine months may be a long time to the waiting mother, but to a toddler, with no concept of time, nine months is an eternity.

One change in policy at some hospitals that many couples have enjoyed is that brothers and sisters are allowed to see the new baby while it is still in the hospital. If Kelly gets to do the very adult thing of going to see her new brother while he is still in the hospital, and look forward to the day when he comes home to be *her* brother, then she is given a role to play in the baby's life.

Kelly can be given an infant-type doll, one with a wobbly head, and can practice diapering alongside her mommy and daddy. She can help choose things for the nursery on shopping trips and "buy" a gift for the baby. As mother packs her suitcase for the hospital several weeks in advance, Kelly can pack her own little suitcase in preparation for her stay at Grandma's while Mom's in the hospital. Involvement in these kinds of activities helps the older child adjust and welcome the newborn into the family.

When I was expecting our second child, I worried that my oldest would go through a second rough adjustment when I returned to work. I knew we would both enjoy my three-month maternity leave together, and feared that she would forget that she used to go to the babysitter's two and a half days a week. I thought she'd blame the new baby as the reason Mommy couldn't stay home anymore.

But friends suggested that I leave Michelle and the new baby periodically at the sitter's during my leave. Then, when the time came for me to go back to work, I would simply need to tell her firmly and lovingly that Mommy works and that I'd be back when the day was over.

Even with all these special efforts, any child is likely to feel some amount of jealousy at sharing Mom and Dad with a new sibling. But it will help to create special times to be shared just with Kelly, to make a special effort to give love and hugs.

The one thing the employed mother doesn't have time to do is paint storybook murals on the nursery walls or knit a cute little layette. I did much of my shopping during lunch hours, and was also glad to accept hand-me-downs and loans from other mothers. Babies do outgrow those first tiny clothes so very fast; it makes little sense to invest a lot of money in them. Buy at yard sales or thrift stores and bring the stuff home and wash it.

But more important than furnishing the nursery and layette is focusing on the fact that we were about to bring another human being into the world. What an exciting, creative undertaking! So many possibilities for learning about life, people, God, and nature! What a chance to instill Christian values and a life outlook that is positive and loving. These are things that the pregnancy books sometimes forget to mention, or that are easy to overlook while concerned about eating good food and finding respectable maternity clothes for the office that don't proclaim "Baby" all over the front.

Stop and think about the miracle of conception—the fascinating way in which a tiny human being grows from just a speck to a squirming seven-and-a-half-pound bundle of love. Being a participant in God's creative process—whether as the mother or the father—is truly one of life's most reward-ing adventures.

Obviously, I was overjoyed to be pregnant, and although I eventually got tired of maternity clothes, basically I breezed through a problem-free pregnancy. As I write this I'm aware of how lucky I was to be so happy, because for many wom-en—the unwed teenager, the forty-two-year-old who thought her family was finished, the woman who has nine months of stomachaches, backaches, leg aches and heart-burn—pregnancy is *not* a good word. I don't have any sim-ple answers for those women. Life isn't fair and some people seem to get more than their share of problems. I had to learn to temper my enthusiasm for my condition out of respect for those to whom pregnancy was a problem. But I do know that God has gifted most of us with the capability of coping with whatever life brings, and when we let him help, he surrounds us with love from caring friends.

5

What Does Labor Really Feel Like?

Soon after our baby was born, lots of friends came to visit. I was intrigued when one friend didn't ask the usual questions like, "How much did the baby weigh?" or, "How long were you in labor?" Rather, she wanted to know, "Melodie, does it *hurt* to have a baby? How does it *really* feel? I've asked other people and they always shrug it off with something like, 'Yes, but you soon forget about it when you see the baby.'"

To be honest, that was precisely what I had wanted to know before I had our first child. In fact, in spite of the prepared childbirth classes we had attended, and in spite of (or because of!) seeing films of actual births, I began to panic—would I lose control and scream obscene things at my husband?

Then we visited a friend in a large university hospital. He had undergone a serious heart operation and had endured weeks of inactivity, daily shots, tubes through his nose, and all sorts of painful tests and probes. My insides drew tight as we walked the halls of that large hospital and saw countless suffering men, women, and children. "If they can live through their ordeals, then I can make it through a few puny hours of labor and delivery. After all, look at the billions of women who have!"

Today, preparing for labor and delivery often begins long before the proverbial midnight ride to the hospital. When our mothers had babies twenty to forty years ago, many knew very little about what to expect in labor. In fact, many of us were born while our mothers were under a kind of "twilight sleep" that was induced just before the baby was born.

One leading obstetrician explained the changes like this: "A hundred years ago, doctors didn't interfere. . . . Then, because of our high mortality . . . rates, we began medicating our patients. We made them totally passive and began to treat them as if they were sick. We threw out the husband and took away the baby.

"Now we need to put it back together again," he went on. "We must undo all the artificial interruptions that were introduced in the name of good obstetrics and give obstetrics back to women."[1]

Prepared childbirth is known by several names—"natural" childbirth and "Lamaze," to name two. But all the terms refer to preparing for childbirth by learning breathing and relaxation techniques that allow the mother to be an active participant in the birth of the baby. They also call for the husband (or a friend) to coach during the labor process. What the classes *don't do* is make childbirth painless or require that the husband actually deliver the baby. Nor does preparing for childbirth necessarily mean a drug-free delivery.

In the past, the father's main purpose during labor and delivery seemed to be pacing the waiting room. Hospitals feared they'd have to take care of fainting husbands as well as the woman having a baby, so men were barred from the delivery and labor rooms.

More fathers are now happily realizing their role in the whole process. As one expectant father, Dwight, said with tongue in cheek, "I was there for the conception; I figure I better be there for the delivery as well!" Even so, participating in delivery is *not* for every couple. The decision is still an individual one, and women need not feel cheated, abandoned, or guilty if the father chooses not to be present.

Many women find that their husbands are not wild at first about the idea of attending childbirth classes. Enlightened ones may go easily, but old ideas about childbirth being women's work die hard. Or sometimes a lack of information about what's involved makes them reluctant.

For instance, I was shocked to find out that my husband thought that if he attended the classes, he would have to do the actual delivering of the baby! After the delivery, Stuart was pleased about his role. "It seemed like the nurses and I did most of the tough work," he said, "and the doctor popped into the delivery room just long enough to catch the baby as it came out! The doctor then had the difficult job of deciding whether it was a boy or girl, and tied a cute little knot for a belly button!"

Stuart was especially happy that prepared childbirth helped me have the baby without any medication. "Sitting through those hours of classes seemed a small price to pay when I saw how alert our little girl was and knew that she didn't have a hangover from drugs."

Most hospitals today welcome the full participation of mother and father; it makes the doctor's job easier if the mother is fully alert and can push to save stress on the baby. And many doctors now agree that the fewer drugs used during delivery, the better, for both the infant and the mother. Mothers who receive no prenatal anesthesia have more alert, responsive babies, which helps in that early infant-parent bonding process.

However, if the mother is unprepared, if labor is prolonged and not progressing, or if the baby is positioned wrong, the mother shouldn't feel guilty about accepting medication.

Sometimes parents who must have a Caesarean section feel "cheated." The mother may feel she was a failure because she was unable to deliver "the natural way." But just as with the acceptance of medication during labor, if a C-section is necessary, parents should not feel guilty but should be grateful that modern medicine made the delivery of a healthy baby possible.

Doctors, hospitals, and parents are "discovering" how to use science and technology, rather than allowing science to use them. God has provided some very natural, effective processes that have worked amazingly well for centuries. He has also provided scientific tools and the skills to use them when necessary. Parents today can be thankful that having a baby is not nearly as life-threatening as it once was.

One of my other concerns was how would I know when real labor began? Would we get to the hospital on time?

I knew from my Lamaze classes and other reading that my uterus had actually been contracting during the last month or two of pregnancy. These normal contractions weren't very painful but were noticeable sensations in the abdomen and back region. These "Braxton-Hicks contractions," as they are called, are sometimes difficult to tell from real labor contractions. But I was told the main thing to remember is that real labor contractions will get longer, stronger, and closer together as time progresses. One test for false labor is to change activities—get up and walk around, take a shower, or cook a meal. Real labor is stimulated by and continues with activity, while false labor fades with activity. That's why many women awake in the night feeling strong contractions, but by the time they've gotten up, dressed, and driven to the hospital, the labor pains have stopped.

On the other hand, I was frying chicken for a big supper, complete with mashed potatoes and gravy, when I started noticing the contractions were coming about ten minutes apart. I thought, "Oh, it's nothing," and kept right on working. After my disappointment the day before when the doctor told me he'd see me "next week," I wasn't about to get my hopes up only to be crushed again. I even ate the big supper I'd prepared—the *last* thing one should do when in real labor.

After supper I lay down for a half hour. During this time the contractions slowed down, so I got up again to wash dishes. My husband was working in his woodshop, convinced this wasn't the real thing. Later I learned that continuing to do light housework like I did probably helped considerably to shorten my labor which lasted only seven hours in all.

The pains kept getting stronger and eventually I lost my wonderful supper. That was when I told Stuart, "This is it. It's the real thing or I wouldn't have thrown up."

He was still unconvinced and began to get ready at a maddeningly slow pace. "I'll just have to turn around and bring you home from the hospital," he complained.

"Honey, they're five minutes apart and if this isn't the real thing, then I'd hate to be around for it!"

We finally arrived at the hospital where my suspicions were confirmed—not first by the examining nurse but by the nurse sitting at the nurse's station. The Lamaze teacher had said experienced nurses can tell if it's real labor just by observing a woman's mood—whether or not she's making jokes and polite chit chat. The nurse watched me pant my way through a stiff pain and said, "This young lady's gonna have a baby." She couldn't have given me a better welcome!

What does an actual labor pain feel like? The best way I can describe it is to have you picture a wave at the ocean. As you watch a wave roll in, you can see it slowly build up volume and momentum until it finally crests and splashes over itself, ebbing and easing back to calmer water. That's the way a labor pain comes and goes. It starts as a mildly uncomfortable backache and stomachache, which feels like something inside is being pulled taut. It builds to an excruciating pain and slowly subsides to a feeling like mild cramps. All of this happens in about fifty to seventy seconds at the peak of active labor, and there is anywhere between one and one-half to five minutes of rest between each pain. If each labor pain is experienced one at a time, like jumping waves, the whole thing becomes a little more manageable. Of course, in early labor, the pains are much milder and come further apart. And each woman experiences pain differently. I recognize that I was very lucky to be in labor only seven hours with a first baby.

It was comforting to have Stuart by my side the whole time, even though the delivery happened so fast we barely had time to gather our thoughts, let alone do all the complicated breathing techniques correctly.

When our baby was finally born and lying on my tummy, I expected to cry and feel an emotional high, like I always did viewing childbirth films. Instead, I was just happy, tired, excited, and interested in how our little girl looked.

I didn't shed my "happy" tears until several days later at home when I tried to say grace before a meal. I started to say, "Thanks, God, for our wonderful new daugh . . ." but I couldn't finish. My cup was so full!

And so our new life with a baby began.

6

Where Do I Go for a Refund?

The nurse placed our little bundle in my arms and closed the door softly. At last! Mommy, Daddy, and three-day-old baby. What a cozy threesome!

That illusion quickly fizzled. Another driver had pulled up too closely behind us in the loading zone and left his car. Stuart had to maneuver the car backward and forward several times to get out. "Dumb driver," he muttered.

Next, a frustrated Stuart braked too sharply to suit me at the first stoplight and I shot him a dirty look. "Well, can't you drive more carefully? Did you forget what a precious bundle we have here?"

"Humph. Nothin' wrong with my driving. But I can see already you're going to be an over-protective mother."

It definitely wasn't going like I had so often fantasized. "Hey, let's pretend we're back at the hospital starting this drive home all over again," I finally said, resorting to an old game we play when things get off on a bad foot. Stuart smiled and relaxed.

As we drove down Main Street, I felt like shouting to the

world, "Hey, we just got out of the hospital. Look at us! We have a brand new baby in this car!"

But the passersby were mostly oblivious. Their world hadn't changed forever. Ours had.

Most first-time parents are overly concerned, like we were, for the well-being of their infant. Pediatrician Dr. Brazelton says that this caring concern will become the foundation for all the energy it takes to care for a little, totally dependent human being. But too often that caring dissolves into feelings of helpless inadequacy at the first signs of fussiness or difficulty.

Dr. Brazelton thinks that anxieties are caused partly by the popular idea that a child is born like a lump of clay; every little thing the parents do or don't do determines the way the child turns out. While it's true that the environment and parents *do* have a tremendous influence, it doesn't start there. According to Dr. Brazelton, each child is born with his or her own personality. He says, "As I observed new babies in the newborn nurseries . . . each infant was a strong individual at birth."[1]

Carol, an acquaintance, had worked as a nurse in the hospital's nursery for four years before having a baby of her own. Even though she had all that experience caring for newborns, she still wanted to have her own little daughter "room in" with her at the hospital from the very first. She explained, "I wanted to learn to know *my* baby, what her patterns were, to see if I had an easy or difficult or average baby." Babies *are* different, just like adults!

It's natural to feel a little clumsy, and inexperienced when caring for a baby. Although I had fed and diapered my sister's kids, I had never been totally in charge of a three-day-old infant. I was so afraid I'd hurt Michelle! Fortunately, babies are just as new at the whole process, and they have short memories. I'm sure she won't remember that first loose, slop-

47

py diaper I put on her. And she won't remember screaming for three minutes as I struggled to close her little undershirt.

Having my mom around to help was great moral support. But accepting help from a mother or mother-in-law depends partly on the relationship you have with her.

Today that decision also depends on her wishes—and availability. Some grandparents say, "We love your children, but we've raised ours." Other grandmothers have jobs they can't leave. And many of us simply live too far away from parents to depend on their help.

I know of one woman who at first refused help from Mother, then later invited it. Her baby was colicky and spent most evenings screaming. Later this woman admitted, "We swallowed our pride and summoned Phil's mother. She was delighted, and what a calming effect she had on all of us, including Jessica!"[2]

Many new mothers are anxious to jump into taking care of things that need doing around the house. Most experts agree: Don't do it. A new mother will regain her strength faster if she gets plenty of rest during the day those first couple of weeks. Nursing goes better, too, if Mom's relaxed and rested. Sleep when the baby sleeps, so that coping with the awake periods, especially the ones that come at 3:00 A.M., is easier.

Although we loved and cared for our baby immensely, there were times I just didn't feel like getting up for the fourth time to see why she was crying. Since I was nursing her, I was usually the one to get up. One time I picked Michelle up out of bed and angrily felt like dropping her just to teach her a "lesson." And sleepily I wondered where I could go for a refund. Immediately I felt terrible that I was capable of even thinking such things.

A number of books on child-raising assured me that having these feelings didn't mean I was a lousy mother. They simply revealed that I was tired, and that my emotions and hormonal balance had been thrown into upheaval by pregnancy and birth. But even knowing this, sometimes all I could do was pray for the patience to survive one more night.

I also found bath time particularly difficult. I was nervous and Michelle reacted with squalls of her own, which only added to my nervousness and desire to "get it over with."

One morning I was bathing her and was irked that a neighbor had interrupted the already troublesome task with a phone call. I commented that I was bathing the baby and the neighbor responded with, "Oh, isn't bath a fun time? They like to play and splash in the water so much."

I wondered what I was doing wrong! I realized one reason I hated bath time so much was that it meant dragging all the bath-time supplies to the kitchen and then, back to the bathroom again. So I found a handy place to keep the supplies in the kitchen. It eliminated half the work of bath time!

Then I started talking and smiling to Michelle, easing her into the tub one foot at a time and allowing her to get used to the temperature slowly. She soon responded with tentative smiles, then active splashing.

I learned to value other tips and comments from friends who'd been through the experience before me. After a particularly rough night when Michelle was two weeks old, I received a card from a high school chum. It said, "Having a new baby is like having every morning be Christmas morning: you just can't wait till she wakes up and you can play with her."

When I first read that, I thought, "Humph, Christmas morning. Her kids are getting too old for her to remember what it was like when they were infants." Then, I don't know if I changed or if the baby changed, but each morning *did* begin to seem like Christmas. Just seeing Michelle alive and well gave such joy that she was like a gift waiting for me in the nursery.

While Stuart and I were very fortunate because we had a baby who didn't seem bothered at all by colic, enough of my friends and relatives had colicky babies to make me wonder about it. After talking with them, I realize there is probably little that is more frustrating or frightening than dealing with a colicky baby. While all babies need to cry—some doctors suggest for a total of three hours a day—babies with colic cry anywhere from eight to twelve hours a day. What exactly is colic and how can parents cope with it?

Dr. Brazelton explains it this way. As the baby cries, her entire body, especially the intestines, become tense and overactive. She gulps down air as she cries. Her stomach is sensitive to the air, and it creates pain, so she cries harder. As the gas in the stomach passes on through the rectum, the pain continues—and so does the crying. By this time the parents have become anxious and frustrated, and the baby also reacts to their tenseness.

But not all crying is related to colic. Dr. Brazelton recommends making every possible attempt to find reasons for the crying and try to quiet the baby. Try feeding, changing, or giving her something to suck on. Try swaddling her securely with a blanket to keep her from frightening herself as she moves. Give her a pacifier or a little sugar water to help her bring up air bubbles, and so on. Some doctors will prescribe sedatives for the baby, but others feel they work only temporarily. The good news for parents who have babies with colic is that practically all babies outgrow the colicky period by three months of age.

Dr. Brazelton further recommends letting the infant cry for fifteen to twenty minutes (if there's nothing seriously wrong); then picking the baby up for ten minutes of comforting, putting her down for twenty minutes more of crying, and so on. This doctor feels that it's not as hard on the infant to cry for periods of fifteen to twenty minutes as it is to be picked up and jostled with "no message coming across but one of frantic tension."[3]

The fact is that some babies are just more sensitive to the

world around them. "They cry more than two hours a day, are difficult to quiet, and they overreact to everything that occurs around them," says Dr. Brazelton.[4] They might cry as much as twelve hours a day. And Dr. Brazelton says the babies will survive, but their parents won't! I know that the parents remember, but the baby doesn't! He also mentions that follow-up studies on some of these overreactive, sensitive infants "show that they often grow up to be extremely bright, alert children."[5]

Despite the many difficulties, new mothers and fathers eventually adapt to all the changes. Baby clutter strewn about the house even begins to look normal. In fact, I soon got so used to packing and unpacking the diaper bag for even the smallest shopping trip that when I did get a chance to go out without the baby, I felt naked without that bag draped over my shoulder! And when we first had a chance to be at home for a few hours while the baby was at my sister-in-law's, the house seemed absolutely empty! It made me realize that in perspective a baby is tiny for only a short time, and children are at home for just a few years. While it's necessary to get relief from the demands of parenting, it's important to try to enjoy the gift of a child every single day. Children really are gifts from God, and the hard work is lightened when we treasure those gifts.

7

Should I Go Back to Work or Not?

In the space of fifteen months, six women at the office where I work became pregnant. Staffers warned, "There must be something in the water here." And the personnel director worried that the women were catching "baby fever" from each other.

However, the mass pregnancies didn't necessarily mean a mass exodus from the office. These six women answered the should-I-go-back-to-work-or-not question in ways as varied as the individuals involved.

It used to be that if a wife worked at all, she worked only until the first child came along, and then she quit a respectable length of time before any telltale bulges revealed her secret. For the record, all except one of my co-workers had worked at least five years at our office before having a baby, and all were over twenty-five years of age. None of them fit the stereotype of a young married woman quitting to have a child within a year after being hired.

Three of the new mothers chose the bedlam and joyful confusion of the nursery over their neat, ordered office desks.

The other three chose to return to paid work after six-week or three-month pregnancy leaves.

Diane, a receptionist for five and a half years, touched off the boom. Diane worked right up to the day before Kelly was born. So when she and husband, Marv, brought their new daughter home, her reaction was, "I couldn't wait to stay at home. I had always looked forward to it and didn't consider anything else."

Marv has a good job as a representative for disposable products, so financial needs aren't a real problem for him and Diane. But Diane feels that people who *think* they have to have a second income to support a family should take a long look at what they miss by not staying home. "When you pay a babysitter, go out for fast foods, bring home convenience foods, buy clothing instead of making it, you don't save that much by working."

Diane admits that she felt housebound when Kelly was four to seven months of age. It seemed Kelly cried and became upset whenever she was left with a babysitter. Diane and Marv attributed her fears to the fact that Marv's job kept him away from home three to four days at a time. "Kelly knows that when Daddy leaves he doesn't come back for a long time, and I think she's afraid that when I leave I won't come back for a long time either." However, doctors have assured Diane that Kelly won't remember her early fears of babysitters.

Now that Kelly is twenty-one months old, Diane has discovered a successful babysitting cooperative where she leaves Kelly simply to have some time to play tennis or go shopping. Ten mothers with small children, who all live close together, belong to the co-op and take turns acting as its secretary. When Diane needs a babysitter, she calls the secretary to find out who "owes" hours to the co-op. Every time she uses babysitting services from the co-op, she then "owes" that same number of hours, and each time she babysits, she acquires hours to her credit to cash in later. Diane explains, "I really like the co-op arrangement because it provides companionship for Kelly and allows me to do things I wouldn't ordinarily get a babysitter for."

The most satisfying result of not going back to paid work has been "being around when Kelly does all her firsts," Diane says with obvious satisfaction. "Watching her grow up is much better than I expected—it's a lot different than babysitting! Knowing that she depends on you for everything and trusts you is extremely gratifying."

However, Diane doesn't think her way is the only one. "Most of my friends work and have young children—some because they think they'd go buggy being home all day, and others because they really have to work. It's really hard on them. All they get done is work and take care of their families."

Roberta and her husband, Gordie, have a fourteen-month-old son, Tim. Roberta worked a little over a year as a secretary and before that attended college while her husband worked as a machinist.

"When we decided to have a family, I knew I would stay home. It does have its frustrating aspects, but I wouldn't have it any other way," Roberta says.

For Gordie and Roberta, there have been definite financial strains with only one income. "There are times when the checkbook is empty, but there's still bread on the table. We've made changes, but it's not impossible to manage," says Gordie. They both feel a couple should talk about how they will live with one income after the baby is born, if they have been dependent on two before. They recognize that many families must have a second income to survive. But those who don't need it should look carefully at whether they're ready to sacrifice time with the child for a job, they say.

Roberta testifies that squeezing the checkbook at the end of the month is worth it. "It would really tear me up to come home from work one day and have the babysitter say, 'Well, your child took his first step today.' Watching Tim develop and grow has been more joyful than I could have ever imagined."

Evie worked four years as an elementary school teacher and then nearly six years as an administrative assistant before quitting to stay home with her infant son, John. "I had enough of a taste of a career that I was really ready to stay home awhile," Evie says, relaxing on the floor with John and her husband, Art.

Art is a pastor and evangelist who travels a good deal. So, although he occasionally cooks, he isn't free to spend much time doing regular household chores. Because of her experience, Evie says that anyone returning to work full time needs to consider seriously the question of how home chores will be divided.

Art and Evie both have been impressed with recent research that stresses the importance of the early bonding that takes place between parents and a child, especially during the crucial first three years. So Evie tries to spend a lot of time with John. "It's the little things I've enjoyed watching him do, not only the big 'firsts.' Hearing him pick up new words, new concepts—especially now at fourteen months—it seems like every day he's understanding more and more. For example, when I ask him if he wants his lunch, he goes right away to his high chair."

Before Evie quit work, she and Art worried some about what the loss of income would mean. "It was really a big drop, but surprisingly we've hardly noticed it," they say. "But then we have been married awhile and have most of our furniture and things." They also feel they haven't had to make any major changes in lifestyle, although they eat out less.

Evie says that she's just beginning to feel a need to get out and stretch herself. "For the first year I just enjoyed being home, but now I'd like to find something to do maybe one day a week on a volunteer basis." To satisfy this need, they have arranged for Art to take over one afternoon a week so Evie can take off to do errands or whatever she wants, without John.

Then there is Lois who chose to bridge the home and office worlds by working part-time, twenty-four hours a week. Before becoming a mother Lois had been working fifteen years, eight of which she had been married to her electrician husband, Wilmer. "I have worked so long I didn't really feel like I could adjust to staying home full-time. We could have handled it financially, but I didn't want to lose out in business skills and the fringe benefits from having worked so long."

Lois is a marketing coordinator and had decided beforehand that if she wasn't allowed to return to work half time, she wouldn't return at all. She didn't want to handle "two full-time jobs." Now she loves her new schedule and her new freedom. She goes to work at 8:30 after leaving seven-month-old Anthony with a babysitter and picks him up again soon after 3:00. "I only miss one meal with Anthony, and for two of the six hours that he's away, he's asleep," she says, pleased.

She also says she hasn't missed any of his "firsts." By working six hours a day, Lois has a four-day week and is home on Fridays. "He seems to save his firsts for me on Fridays! I only wish I would have worked part-time like this a year before I had Anthony."

What does she like least about her arrangement? "Getting him and his gear all ready to go in the morning!" Lois found it difficult to schedule the traditional morning bath for Anthony, so she and Wilmer both bathe Anthony in the evening after supper. Then he's ready to "conk out." "This way Wilmer

56

gets to help out in what many fathers miss. If I was home full-time, he'd probably be less involved with Anthony."

Lois does feel at a disadvantage working part-time. She says, "I don't know as much about what's going on, and I don't learn to know people as well." But in all, she feels she has the best of both worlds—"I appreciate Anthony more when I get home than if I were here all day."

Betty Jo and her husband, Joe, knew that if they ever wanted to start a family, she'd have to continue working full-time as she had the five years they'd been married. She shares, "We knew that it was true that if you wait to have a child until you can afford it, you'll never have one." After her first baby was born, Betty Jo took a three-month leave of absence from her job as secretary, returned part-time for one month, and then returned full time.

"Originally I would have loved to quit if I could have, but now I'm kind of glad I couldn't. My aunt warned, 'Oh, you're going to miss out on everything.' But I thought, 'Well, I'll just learn to appreciate him that much more then.'" Incidentally, Betty Jo says she hasn't missed many of Travis's firsts at all. Proudly, she claims, "Travis seems to try most of his new things in the evening when I'm home. He really looks forward to me coming home"—a fact her babysitter confirms.

"A child really does place a lot of demands on you and your time. But I feel the time I do spend with Travis is more relaxed and concentrated. I enjoy it more than if I'd been with him all day. It does get a little hectic around supper," she smiles.

For Betty Jo an important factor to consider when deciding if the mother will return to work is whether she really likes her job. "If she resents giving up her job, her baby would be better off if she worked."

None of the previously mentioned couples seriously considered having the husband stay home to be primary care-giver for the child. Although Glenda and David, parents of ten-month-old Erica, talked about it and Dave says, "I would enjoy that," like the others, they never gave it serious thought either. Glenda returned to her job as bookkeeper full-time after only a six-week leave because her employer needed the position filled and requested that she do so.

Glenda likes working at the office to "be with other people and feel like you accomplish something each day. Sometimes it's harder to see the immediate results of raising a child."

Deciding to go back was a difficult decision for Dave and Glenda. "One day I'd say I was quitting, and the next day I'd say I'd go back. I floundered back and forth like that for awhile, and finally my brother gave what I thought was sensible advice. 'If you don't know what to do, why don't you go back to work and see if you like it and then you can always quit if you don't. That would be easier than going out and trying to find a new job if you quit and then decided you want to work.' "

Dave and Glenda say that the longer one works, the harder it is to quit. "You build up vacation time, seniority, and pay. Sometimes it's best not to think too hard and debate too long about your decision. At any rate, you shouldn't let it stop you from having a child. There's no way to put a dollar value on what Erica's brought to us," says Dave.

He also comments, "I bet you'd get a very different viewpoint on this if you'd interview people one generation back— parents or grandparents. Many feel so strongly against mothers of young children working. But Glenda's own mother now says she thinks Glenda is doing just as good a job mothering as she could by staying home all day."

Both Dave and Glenda think the number one question a couple should ask themselves if the wife is returning to work should be: "Is the husband willing to do his share around the house?" Otherwise, they caution, the wife may end up working eighteen to twenty-four hours a day.

Even when the chores are shared, Glenda admits that evenings can get hectic. "You want to play with the baby, so you have to wait to do the wash until after you put her to bed. Then you stay up until midnight doing the laundry because you need the diapers the next day."

About a year and a half after this baby boom at my office, I got pregnant. Suddenly the "back to work or not" question became very personal. Gone was the theorizing about "quality time" and "being fulfilled." Suddenly it didn't matter what Glenda and Lois and Diane had done. What should I do? What was right for us?

One night we sat down and figured out all of our expenses for the year. It was not a plush budget, but rather a no-frills, generic budget filled with basics. Then we looked at Stuart's salary and calculated exactly how many hours I would need to work in order to meet our obligations. We figured the minimum number to be something like sixteen hours a week. Since my office offered no fringe benefits for those working under twenty hours a week, we decided that I'd ask for the possibility of working twenty hours a week and get the benefit of vacations, holidays, medical and life insurance, and retirement benefits. We looked at our child-care options, my interests, Stuart's availability to be home most evenings, and what kind of parents we wanted to be.

Now I know what Betty Jo meant by suppertime being a little hectic. And what it's like to want to play with the baby when the dishes need washing. And what a hassle it is to get out the door in the morning. I also know with Roberta that raising a child is "more joyful than I could have ever imagined."

Somehow I feel we've each made the "right" decision for now, considering circumstances, jobs, and personalities.

God has given people an enormous capacity for adapting to new circumstances and opportunities.

As Glenda says of her decision to return to work full-time, "It gives you a really good feeling to know you can do it if you have to or want to." That statement applies equally to staying home—it feels good to know it's possible to survive living with a baby all day.[1]

8

What If Johnny Likes His Sitter Better than He Likes Me?

The success stories of superwomen make me a little sick. Working mothers who make $50,000 a year, raise brilliant kids, keep a spotless house, and throw huge dinner bashes aren't the women I know.

But I do know many mothers who work full- or part-time, make enough money to keep the bill collector off the doorstep, and are happy, well-adjusted persons (if a bit harried). Their children are cheerful and well-adjusted, too. It takes a lot of energy, organization, and family cooperation, but as one says, "You can do just about anything you really want to."[1]

And these women are the first to tell you that being a working mother is not for everyone. It's waking at 5:20 A.M. and punching the snooze alarm for a few more minutes of precious sleep. It's being careful not to bang the pots and pans while making breakfast so the kids stay asleep. It's packing two or three lunches and then a diaper bag and hoping the baby doesn't cry while you're in the shower. It's taking a few minutes to cuddle the toddler in your lap before rushing to dress, diaper, and feed her. It's leaving the house at

7:45 A.M. with the knowledge that the hardest part of the day is over.

This, or a variation of it, is the scene in six million North American homes with full- or part-time working mothers and preschool children. The vast majority of these mothers, and their husbands, are deeply concerned about having good day-care arrangements.

"Will my working hurt my child?" mothers ask. I think there are several key factors that suggest an answer. Do I feel good about myself and my work? Do I feel good about our child-care arrangements? Do we both, mother and father, make a concentrated effort to give children focused attention when at home? If the answers to these questions are all yes, then most likely the children will not be psychologically damaged by the mother working outside the home.

I find it interesting that little fuss is made about whether a father's work damages his relationship with his children. Sometimes, when I'm home alone with Michelle, out of the blue she'll say, "I want my daddy." Children miss their fathers as well as their mothers, but too often we don't worry about that. Columnist Letty Pogrebin reported one doctor's findings. In one study, children were asked about their feelings about their parents' jobs. These children expressed "almost as many bad feelings about fathers leaving for work as about mothers."[2]

Perhaps it would be helpful not to think in terms of whether a working mom is "bad" or "good" for children. Being a good mom or a bad mom is related to how a woman feels about herself and her children. It's related to how she understands God's leading in her life at that particular time. One psychologist reported that "studies of elementary school children show that . . . the best adjusted children have mothers who are satisfied with what they are doing."[3]

In addition to the mother's self-perception, good child-care arrangements are also crucial to the ongoing emotional health of the whole family, and to how one feels about working. But selecting the right sitter can be particularly overwhelming to new parents who barely understand their own new roles! How do you find the *right* care? How do you root out someone who fits your style of parenting and your value system?

Many women I know rely on personal contacts—asking friends and relatives if they know of good, available sitters. This is also a good way to find someone with Christian values and a Christian lifestyle.

Another way is to ask specific questions like, "What would you do if my child takes all the toilet paper off the roll?" Or, "What would you do if my child bites another child, throws food," and so on.

When screening possible sitters, notice how the person relates to children. One woman said that as she was interviewing applicants, she noted one prospective sitter "who was so cold she never said one word to Jennifer, including goodbye."[4]

On the other hand, mothers sometimes worry in reverse. What if Johnny starts to like the sitter better than he does me? I remember how unnerving it was one day when I put ten-month-old Michelle on the living room floor at the sitter's house. She crawled immediately to the sitter's ten-year-old son and pulled at his legs, saying "Ma Ma." I was glad I had read that a baby often uses the words "Da Da" and "Ma Ma" to get someone to do something—in this case to pick her up!

So, what are the options for child care? The first option many people desire is a private babysitter who comes to the home. The child has the least disruption to his life that way, and theoretically, the amount of time the sitter spends with the child is greater than it is in other day-care situations.

The drawbacks of this option are: (1) there aren't many people available to do this kind of sitting anymore; (2) if there are no siblings, the child doesn't have the companionship of other children; and (3) it's usually expensive.

Another option is to have a relative—a grandmother, aunt

or great aunt, sister or sister-in-law—care for the child. Because family bonds are involved, a relative normally takes a more natural, ongoing interest in the child.

However, many families do not have relatives available to babysit due to distance, jobs, or other interests. Also, the mother and father may feel especially jealous and guilty if the child seems to prefer the relative over Mom or Dad.

In many communities, there are mothers who make a full-time job out of caring for several preschoolers in addition to their own children. If the total number of children who are in the home all day is relatively small—say two to four—this can be a very good option, because this situation provides playmates and a true home atmosphere. However, when interviewing this type of care-giver, parents should carefully observe if she is too busy or involved with her own children and household to give proper attention to others.

Among some larger corporations, one trend is to provide company-run day-care services. The advantages are obvious—less time and expense in commuting, more control over the quality of care.

Yet another key option is a commercially operated day-care center, usually for children over two. Here are some things to look for:

- Does the center have a low staff turnover? It's important for a child to have consistent relationships with the people at a center.
- Does the center seem to welcome parent involvement and visits, freely answering questions?
- Does the staff seem to like kids? Do they talk and play with them?
- Does the place seem safe—equipment in good repair, covers on electrical outlets, things like that?
- Are there places where children can get away from the group—pillows in a corner where a child can have some quiet moments to himself if he wants?

- Is there a good safe place to play outside, as well as in?
- How do you *feel* about the place? Would you enjoy spending four to eight hours there?[5]

Once you have chosen the best day care for your child, watch for signs indicating whether or not the child is happy. For instance, does she seem somber or sad? Is he more anxious and agitated? Has she gone back to thumbsucking, bedwetting, or wanting a bottle? Does he withdraw, wanting to spend more time in bed and refusing to get up in the morning? While all these signals could be related to other problems, they may be linked to an unpleasant day-care experience. Here are some suggested solutions:

- Take ten to fifteen minutes to spend concentrated time with the child each morning. This may mean getting up earlier, but if it helps the child feel more in touch with his parents, it will be well worth it.
- Go earlier to the center or the babysitter's and stay with the child while he or she is adjusting to the new environment.
- Talk to the babysitter or the staff people to find out if they've noticed what in particular may be bothering Jill. Maybe an older child has been pestering her, or maybe she feels "out of it" because she's the only one in diapers.

Most women need and seek some regular relief from full-time mothering responsibilities. Whether that relief comes in the form of a job away from home, or by forming a babysitting cooperative with neighbors, or by leaving the infant at Grandma's house several hours a week, most mothers find that regular time away from baby is a lifesaver.

That may be hard to explain to a one-year-old, but some day I hope my daughter will read this and understand:

Dear Daughter,

If you could talk, I imagine one of your most-asked questions would be: "Mother, if you love and enjoy me so much, why do you leave me to go to work?"

I ask myself that sometimes, too. In fact, every morning when I close the door at the babysitter's house, even though you're happy there, something inside me cringes.

The bottom line is financial. Although we have only a modest home and furnishings, we *do* want to provide a pleasant home in a nice community for you. I think I'm like most mothers who have paid jobs—I'm not working for the luxury of extras, but for the groceries, the house payment, your shoes, the gas, and the insurance. I'm working because I love you, and I want to help provide for you, given our circumstances.

Frankly, I feel you benefit too, even though the goodbyes are hard for me and the hours probably seem long for you. You have learned to expand your circle of love far beyond just Mommy and Daddy. Your sitter has taught you words, motions, activities, skills, and to enjoy new foods and new friends. Her children are like a big brother and big sister to you, and you look forward to "going bye bye" in the morning.

And I have to say I look forward to "going bye bye," too. If you're ever a mother, I hope you'll understand what a relief it is to let someone else diaper, calm, and entertain an infant for a few hours a day. By working just part-time, I feel I have the best of both worlds—I get to spend significant amounts of time with you, but I also get adult stimulation and conversation and a chance to focus beyond you.

I try to compensate by doing the things all good mothers do. I give you lots of cuddles, affirmation, changes of activity, and attention, *and* I require that you spend time playing by yourself occasionally. I don't want to "spoil" you by overindulging you in a futile effort to make up for lost time!

I'm exhausted many evenings, and so, feel relieved when

you snuggle in your bed for sleep. That is time for me and Daddy to recharge our energies for another full day of giving.

It's not a perfect solution or life. But being a full-time mother has its disadvantages, too. I'm not sure what a perfect life would be—or if humans were meant to have one on this earth. But I do know several things. God continues to give me strength. He continues to help us meet our financial obligations. You are happy at the sitter's and you're happy when I pick you up. I am happy at the office *and* at home with you.

In praying for direction for our lives together, your father and I feel like this is the only option for right now, and that God has blessed us with a caring, loving, competent child. So we are trusting God that this is right for you, right for us.

With all my love,
Mommy

9

Breastfeeding Was Beautiful Until My Baby Went on Strike

"Am I doing the right thing?" I chewed my lip and hurried off the babysitter's front porch on my way back to work after my three-month maternity leave. I wondered if Michelle would starve herself, or if she would be happy with the bottles I had left for her.

When I got to work, a knowing co-worker quipped, "Who cried the most this morning?"

"Well, it wasn't Michelle," I said, flashing a braver smile than I felt.

The truth was I hadn't actually cried either. It felt good to be returning to the professional world. It would be good to shuffle papers all day instead of diapers. And I knew I was lucky in that it was just a half-time job.

But I agonized over how nursing would work out. I knew many working moms and many breastfeeding moms, but I didn't know personally any who were combining the two. Originally I had planned to have Michelle weaned from the breast by the time I returned to work, but I had never antici-pated how enormously satisfying that relationship would be to me.

About three weeks before returning to work, I armed myself with formula and sat down to acquaint Michelle with a bottle. This was how the "books" said to wean a baby when returning to work. I was to introduce a bottle several weeks ahead of time, and gradually eliminate the number of breast-feedings until she was receiving the same number of bottle feedings that she'd get from the babysitter.

Well, Michelle hadn't read the same books. And she wasn't about to be fooled by that old bottle when she knew there was something available that was much sweeter and more comforting. After fighting with her for about fifteen minutes, I gave in—and felt terrible. Terrible that I was returning to work and had to force the bottle on her, and terrible that I had given in to her demand. Was I spoiling her already? How was I going to get her used to the bottle so she wouldn't starve on her first day with the babysitter?

I told a friend about my dilemma. She advised taking a longer lunch hour to go to the babysitter's house and nurse Michelle. It sounded sensible, except that I usually fed Michelle when she was hungry rather than according to some inflexible, arbitrary schedule. She also slept when she felt like it. What would happen if I went to the babysitter's at lunch, Michelle was napping, and I was due back at the office for a one o'clock high-level staff meeting? While I had a very understanding boss, I didn't think it would go over very well to say, "Sorry, I was nursing."

I asked our doctor for his opinion. Wisely he informed me that babies often refuse to take bottles from their own mothers because they associate mother's smell with breast milk. If the baby smells breast milk, she's not going to be satisfied until she gets that! "Try letting someone else give her a bottle," he advised.

On a visit to my mother's, I prepared a bottle and stayed out of the room while Mom tried her hand at feeding Michelle. "She might smell me," I warned. Well, she proceeded to satisfy a very hungry little girl, who gulped down four ounces and wanted more. I was happy. Now, at least, I could relax about my plans to return to work. But I felt a little left out. Michelle could survive without me after all.

I thought the toughest part was over until 11:00 A.M. on that first day back. Suddenly my breast milk "let down." Of course, I had prepared for that by inserting pads into my nursing bra before leaving that morning so no embarrassing leaks showed. But I started to feel more and more uncomfortable as the day wore on. I nursed Michelle to relieve the pressure, just as soon as I got home and as often as she wanted throughout the evening. But even that wasn't enough to use up all the milk. I went to work the next morning already full and more uncomfortable. How would I make it until 4:30? I had tried manual expression of the milk, but that was slow and ineffective. And I knew about breast pumps, but most were expensive.

I confided in another friend. She suggested I call La Leche League, an organization providing information and moral support for nursing women, because I could rent a breast pump from them to see how it went. When I picked one up that evening, the La Leche League leader was sympathetic and helpful. "You can get clogged ducts and breast infections awfully fast if you don't empty your milk regularly," she advised.

The pump helped a lot the next day. Because Michelle was on formula during the day, I discarded my milk and didn't worry about storing it. But since then I've heard of women who have found all sorts of ingenious ways to keep the milk cool so it could be taken home and fed to baby the next day—packing a thermos with ice, storing it in the office refrigerator, or even getting permission to store it inside a soft drink machine.

In the days and weeks that followed, I learned I could somewhat regulate my milk supply by cutting back drastically on the amount of liquids I drank about twelve hours before returning to work on the days I worked eight hours. Then I resumed drinking extra liquids on my days off to build back the supply. On days when my own supply ran low, I supplemented with bottle feedings in the evening. That was often handy, especially if we went out and it was inconvenient to nurse.

For about two months, Michelle went handily back and forth between me and the bottle. I was elated. Then, without warning, she went on "strike." Instead of refusing the bottle, she started refusing to nurse, especially if she got distracted during a feeding. I was devastated, although I could barely admit it. I had secretly gloated over the fact that I could still do something for my little daughter that my very competent babysitter couldn't. Now she was cutting that one very special link.

The La Leche League leader said Michelle's refusal to nurse was caused by nipple confusion, going back and forth between bottle and breast. Such behavior sometimes is brought on by teething, by a cold, or just because it's easier for the baby to get milk from a bottle. She said some mothers try to feed their babies when they're sleeping. Others just try to tough it through.

I hated fighting with Michelle to nurse, but I couldn't deny she was asserting an obvious preference for the bottle. I debated a whole weekend, trying to get her to nurse, and then usually giving in with a bottle. I decided my own ambivalence was probably the most unsettling to her, and quietly nursed her for the last time on a Sunday morning. "Just the first in a series of apron strings to be cut," my head said.

The breast pump eased me through the next several days of discomfort, but even this rather abrupt weaning wasn't nearly as uncomfortable as I had feared.

During this time of change for me and Michelle, it would

71

have helped me so much to be able to share my concerns more frequently with a support group like the La Leche League. Unfortunately, my hectic schedule often conflicted with their meetings. But I was thankful to God that I had been able to continue nursing for as long as I did. As the La Leche League believes, "One day of nursing is better than not at all; one week is better than a day; one month is better than a week," and so on. Although breastfeeding after returning to work was somewhat bothersome—taking the breast pump to work, getting rid of the milk, wearing bra pads and special clothes—it eased my transition back to work.

For those first two months, the best part of my day was picking up my nuzzling, anxious infant. While I breastfed Michelle, I forgot about schedules, reports, meetings, and even about making supper for forty-five minutes. I would become completely unprofessional and would enjoy unashamedly what to me was one of the nicer things about having a baby. And nursing Michelle also established a good habit that continues even now that she is weaned. Usually, the first half hour or so that I'm home is still Michelle's. We play, eat, or sometimes just rock, but most importantly, we still share that special time.

There is no reason why mothers can't try to combine nursing and working. But it is important for those who attempt to do it all to remember that each infant is different, and that there are varying degrees of success.

Someday I'll tell Michelle about the very first boycott she staged. I couldn't help thinking she was already an independent little female. But although she could thrive without my milk, she let it be known she still needed what her father and I could give best: lots of love. And it is our hope that the love we give will, in turn, help her understand a little about God's love.

10

Terrible Toddlers
and Other Self-fulfilling Prophecies

One day when Stuart, Michelle, and I were at a lake, a little boy about two years old strayed twenty-five to thirty feet from his mother. Cautiously he began sharing pails and shovels with our little girl. Then without warning, the stranger threw a handful of sand into Michelle's eyes. Quickly the boy's mother came and apologized profusely, scolded the little boy, and shrugged, "Terrible twos, you know."

"Terrible twos." Is it a myth, an excuse parents use for a misbehaving child? Or is it a reality that toddlers do go through some developmental stages that make living especially difficult?

In some ways, I hate to use the label for fear of perpetuating the mythical aspects. In reality, "twos" are probably not much more terrible than kindergarten homesickness or teenage years. Not all two-year-olds do all the things the developmental books talk about. Nor does all child development happen at the suggested "proper" times.

A North American toddler is really trying to accomplish a number of amazing feats all at one time. For one, he's learning to master the English language which, according to linguists, is a very difficult language to learn. He may also be in the process of breaking a lifelong habit like giving up a pacifier, or bottle, or thumb. (I gained new sympathy for my daughter's attachment to her bottle when I tried to quit drinking coffee.) He is trying hard to remember not to wet his pants, not to spill his cup, and to share his toys. Compounded with that, he may be trying to get used to a new little baby—one who can't play, who cries a lot, and who seems to get more of Mom's attention than he does. No wonder some toddlers have a difficult time and seem to enjoy making life hectic for Mom and Dad!

A two-year-old is struggling for independence while also wanting to cling to babyhood. That is a basic fact of life for the toddler. On one hand, the child wants to do things herself, but on the other hand, she still wants Mommy to hold her. This struggle colors so much of what she does and feels that it's worthwhile to keep it in mind.

One child-care specialist says that "when your toddler clings to you, she is letting you know that there are certain anxieties and fears present in a situation."[1] She needs your special attention for a little while.

Michelle was in this precarious, clingy stage when we visited Great-Grandma for Christmas one year. (We live six hundred miles from my grandmother and don't get to see her as often as we would like.) Her house was dark and old-fashioned, which looked strange to Michelle; and Great-Grandma was wearing thick glasses. For the first ten minutes, Michelle clung to me so firmly I couldn't even take off my coat. So I just held her and talked to my grandmother awhile, without prying Michelle away or shaming her. Finally Great-Grandma remembered a box of old toys that I had played with when I was a little girl. At the mention of toys, Michelle climbed out of my lap and started thawing out. She shyly took some toys and after a short time she was even ready to give Great-Grandma a kiss.

A clinging child can be an embarrassment, especially when you want to impress relatives who don't see the child very often. But it's usually best to let the child proceed at her own pace, although Mother can make suggestions like, "Maybe Grandpa will take you out to see his doggy."

However, a child who clings most of the time is doing so for a very important reason. Here are several possibilities: perhaps the child is worried about a crisis in the family or possibly his regular routine has been interrupted; maybe she feels pressured to grow up faster than she can handle, or maybe she is expressing the fear that comes with increased responsibility as she grows up.[2] Whatever the reason, try to recognize your child's times of insecurity and make a special effort to show your love during them.

Two-year-olds can also be quite negative. It seems like their favorite word is "No!" A noted psychiatrist says that this "two-year-old negativism" is crucial for normal child development. It is one of the ways each of us separates ourselves psychologically from our parents.[3] It's also important for working mothers to keep in mind that toddler negativism and tantrums are probably *not* related to their working.

How do you distinguish between normal negativism and outright defiance? If a two-year-old deliberately does something that he knows is wrong, that is different from simple negativism and should be dealt with. On the other hand, punishing a child for a lot of "nos" is pointless. Kids soon learn to manipulate their parents. If Sandra knows she gets lots of attention by refusing to wear shoes in the house, she'll continue to force the issue. However, if it doesn't really matter and the house is kept warm enough, it becomes one less way she can manipulate.

A toddler needs and wants some limits set. An indecisive parent quickly conveys his indecision to the child, and the child feels confused and at a loss. However, the limits and discipline need to be set according to each child, parent, and situation. That's what makes parenting hard—there aren't many answers that work all the time.

Living with negativism and some tantrums seems to be a natural part of raising a toddler. So is worrying about potty training, one of the bigger issues for a toddler, which often consumes a lion's share of young parents' thoughts and efforts.

When preparing to potty train, a parent should look for certain signs of the child's *readiness* to use the toilet. My sister advised me that she soon learned that trying to train a child who was still taking a bottle was quite useless. The child was simply drinking too much liquid to be expected not to wet her pants. Other signs to look for include when the child demonstrates an interest in the toilet, and likes to imitate adults in other activities like brushing teeth, or shaving, and when the child develops the verbal skills she needs to be able to understand conversations about using the toilet.

Let me offer another suggestion that I've read repeatedly and agree with: don't begin training during another major transition period in your child's life. Is the family moving, expecting another child, anticipating a major trip? Has the child just accomplished weaning? Has Mother just gone back to "work"? Take a break! As much bother as diapers are, it's less bother than a complete change of clothes every time the child "forgets."

Once the decision to potty train has been made, the child's sitter can be a tremendous help. I know one working mother who noticed all of a sudden that little Elizabeth hadn't had a single accident in over two weeks. The mother was pleased but somewhat puzzled by this success. Then she learned the sitter had been paying special attention to the "training." Parents just need to talk with the sitter and make sure they agree with her methods.

Another major issue for the toddler may be getting used to the arrival of a second child. Mothers today who postpone having children until they're older often plan their families closer together. Mary Lou told me that for the whole first year she was at home with two children born two years apart, she sometimes wondered if an outside world even existed! "But after that, the children were such companions to each other all through childhood that the first difficult year was worth it."

That said, how does one prepare a toddler for an addition to the family? Here are several suggestions:

Do tell the child about the expected birth several months before delivery, but not too soon. Remember a toddler has no concept of nine months! But he should hear the news from his parents before friends and relatives begin asking him about it.

If the hospital permits it, have the child visit mother and baby in the hospital before they come home. Partings will be difficult, but the whole concept of "Mommy's in the hospital," and "you have a new baby sister" will become so much more real that even tearful goodbyes are worth it.

When Mom gets home from the hospital, try to let someone else settle the new baby, while Mom spends some time alone with the toddler. There may be some temporary whining, clinging, or other babyish behavior for awhile. The toddler may revert to thumbsucking, drinking a bottle, or pants-wetting. Don't tell him he must grow up now that he is a big brother. Instead, give the child the attention he needs.

Giving both children the attention they need can be difficult though. It may take months until the toddler feels secure enough in his new role that he's content to play by himself while mother rocks the baby, for example.

Play is the toddler's major activity. It's his work, what he does with his day. But children vary a lot as to how well they're able to play by themselves. Naturally, if there is an older brother or sister in the house, toddlers are usually content for longer periods without Mom. Most activities are more fun when there're two. But it's important for parents to be

77

involved in child's play at times too. It's unrealistic to expect a toddler to be able to find things to do by himself for long stretches of time.

Although toys and games that are purchased can be convenient and fun they can also be expensive. So a child's play shouldn't be dependent on them. Try the following ideas, keeping in mind that a toddler enjoys making things work—being able to make things happen by what he does.

For instance, playing in water—whether it's the bathtub, backyard pool, or kitchen sink—pouring water back and forth from one cup to another, dipping out soap bubbles with a spoon, or simply splashing is great entertainment for a toddler.

Although play dough is a mess and generally recommended only for older children, try letting the toddler use it on a low table with plenty of newspaper on the floor. She may need some guidance at first about how to make little balls, use cookie cutters, make baskets, long ropes and so on, but it soon becomes a favorite pastime.

And, of course, big boxes are fun. With a little imagination they can become houses, cars, trains, or a variety of other vehicles, dwellings, and creatures. Just let the toddler color to her heart's content on the sides.

It's always fun to go outside—after the hassle of putting on shoes, coats, and hats. The fresh air does mother and toddler both some good. A walk around the block or down the lane provides a change of scenery. And jumping off low platforms, running, pushing strollers or wagons can all be vents for pent-up steam.

Try to avoid activities that are too complicated and frustrating for the toddler. Generally, when making things out of paper or material, the parent ends up doing all the work and clean-up himself! Kids' TV shows, books, and other parents can be great sources of ideas for a variety of simple playthings.

Many mothers have found that play groups, mothers'

groups, or drop-in centers provide relief from the harried days of raising toddlers. In some communities there are organized, formal "Mothers' Centers" that offer a professional staff of care-givers for the children, with planned activities for the mothers. Other groups are loosely organized, meeting in a church nursery, basement, or home. The toddlers play while the mothers watch nearby, have coffee, and share experiences.

Or it may be that a job outside the home provides all the relief one needs. At coffee break, moms-on-the-job compare notes on child-rearing just like the stay-at-home kind.

While toddlers can be difficult to live with, on the flip side they also surprise us with unexpected moments of charm. When Michelle was in her "excessively clingy" stage, Stuart, Michelle, and I were visiting my Uncle Dan. I hardly recognized him as he sat across the room. Felled by a stroke, this once capable, alert man was now sober and weak, and having difficulty recognizing me and my family.

Michelle was eyeing my uncle as well. In her arms she clutched a brand new stuffed puppy, a Christmas gift. She was usually quite shy around strangers.

But I wanted so badly to get through to my uncle, to cause some glimmer of recognition. It was a wild shot; Michelle would never leave my side. But I decided to try anyway. "Go show Uncle Dan your new puppy dog," I whispered. "Go on, show Uncle Dan." Slowly Michelle toddled the eight steps across the room and held out her precious new toy to Uncle Dan. With his good arm, he reached out to receive it, a childish grin breaking on his face. His eyes glistened, and I knew that something had touched him.

Suddenly temper tantrums, messy living rooms, and all the shouted "nos" faded in importance. Children have an uncanny way of doing just the right thing at the right time, of showing us a bit of God's love and grace. And that's part of what makes raising a toddler worth it after all.

11

When God Says, "Wiggle"

A four-year-old friend, Jennifer, rocked back and forth on her heels. "What time is it when an elephant sits on your pence [fence]?" she asked me with an impish grin.

"I don't know," I played along.

"Time to get a new pence," she squealed in delight.

Even though she'd cracked a laugh out of me, I began to wonder how I would ever intellectually survive the preschool years if I had to listen to silly elephant jokes all day long.

For the first two years of their lives, we coax kids to talk, wish they were out of diapers, and worry about why they won't give up the bottle or pacifier. Then we spend the next three years trying to get them to stop asking questions for just five minutes, pleading with them not to run to the potty every fifteen minutes for a false alarm, and secretly wishing for that old plug to keep them quiet.

In spite of all that, the preschool years are a precious stretch between babyhood and school. Children won't always be little. So we need to stop and take time to enjoy them while they are.

Viola is a mother who especially enjoys preschoolers. She

says, "Take time to do things with the children. We live near a woods, so we take walks in the woods. It's one thing to walk in the woods by yourself, and quite another to walk with a child. We walk quietly, listening for the sounds." In the city, listen for unusual street and human sounds when exploring with a preschooler.

Taking long walks in the park may seem a little farfetched to working moms. "It's all I can do just to get the housework done in my time off. How am I supposed to sew cutesy little puppets and blow bubbles with all I have to do?"

It all depends on scheduling. Not that it's possible to run a preschooler's world like a boot camp. Some couples have found it helps just to schedule their evening mealtime a half hour or an hour later, in order to spend time with the children before preparing supper. If the kids are too hungry to wait, let them have a nutritious snack, like fruit or carrots. If that spoils their appetite for supper, so what, as long as it's nourishing.

In the time that is available, practice really listening to the preschooler. Look her straight in the eyes and give her your full attention. A child, like all of us, needs to sense her own self-worth. Meeting Mary eye-to-eye will make her feel important and will nurture a good self-image.

Children pick up attitudes very quickly. They need to know that they *can* and *do* contribute to Mommy and Daddy's happiness. We can show them our joy by always greeting them in the morning and after work with a big smile and special nickname. We can reserve discussions about conflicts for private times, perhaps when the children are sleeping— even if they don't understand the conversation, they sense the tension. We can express our positive feelings verbally and frequently tell them how much they help to make us happy. Mothers' and fathers' attitudes toward their children are really some of the most influential factors in the children's development—a fact that is both frightening and challenging. When sharing time with a child keep your overall goals in mind—What kind of person do we want the child to become? What values are important? This can ease the frustration when there's been one elephant joke too many.

Preschoolers need lots of physical activity. If they don't get it, they become restless, demanding, and start getting into things.

One grandmother who is much wiser than I'll probably ever be likes to tell parents, "Getting into things is not naughtiness. Curiosity is one of the child's gifts from God. Curiosity is a great driving force that God gives to the child so he will use his God-given senses and powers. If he wasn't curious, he wouldn't learn. If God says, 'Wiggle,' should I demand sitting still?"[1]

Play is the preschooler's work or job. It occupies most of his waking hours. So preschoolers constantly need something to do. But that doesn't mean that an adult has to suggest and direct his activities *all* the time. A preschooler needs opportunities to find things to do on his own, in order to fully develop his five senses.

Preschoolers need a variety of items to play with, but toys needn't be expensive or elaborate. The best playthings allow for unstructured play, like building blocks, crayons, a sandbox, simple dolls. These the child can play with creatively. If four- and five-year-olds have access to crayons, paints, and modeling clay, they often come up with surprising works of art. But don't force Bobby to follow the lines of the coloring book. Encourage him to draw pictures of his own. It doesn't matter if the picture doesn't "look like anything." A child's creative urges can easily be discouraged if he feels his pictures must always make sense to an adult.

Three- to five-year-old children are just beginning to think for themselves. The ideas that pop into four-year-old Sherry's head give her much self-satisfaction.[2] Her curiosity is a most wonderful tool. With it she discovers all kinds of things about herself and her world. Sometimes a child's curiosity even takes her "out of this world," as was the case with Winifred.

Winifred came running to tell her mother that she had seen an elephant sitting on top of a fence post. A friend who was visiting in the home asked the mother after Winifred left, "Don't you call that a lie?" The mother answered, "No, just imagination." The child had probably seen an elephant in a book and in her mind made an original image out of the elephant and the fence post.[3]

So it's important to take time to look at the world through the eyes of a preschooler. Wonder with your preschooler at nature. Attend to her jabber, the rhymes and songs she invents. It can open windows to a delightful, magical world.

It's also important to listen to the preschooler. I was visiting with a friend, Sara. Three-year-old Joseph interrupted with a story he was bursting to tell. I was intrigued as she asked Joseph to wait just a minute till Mommy was finished with her story, then he could tell his. And she kept her promise. She finished her thought, then Joseph proceeded to entertain us both with a fanciful tale about some invented friend.

Another preschooler, four-year-old Todd, told his mother, "Look, Mommy, the sun is playing hide-and-seek with the clouds!" Normal, everyday occurrences appear magical and game-like to children of this age.

Preschoolers' alert minds also need stimulation. Reading to them does much to foster this mental stimulation and contributes to feelings of emotional attachment to parents.

Since books and records are so expensive to buy, borrow from the public or church library. A trip to the public library is a special treat for preschoolers. The thought of going to a large building that isn't routinely visited is exciting in itself. Many libraries also have special reading nooks and interesting play corners designed to stimulate a child's imagination. And I know that Michelle feels so "grown up" when she's allowed to choose any book she wants.

But don't push Regina to begin reading on her own too soon. Sometimes parents feel that the preschooler must begin reading before she starts school. This puts too much pressure on the child and can make the child resent school before it ever begins. It's enough for preschoolers to receive stimulation from books simply by seeing the pictures and being read to. But be sure to alternate quiet, thinking activities with more strenuous physical activities and games. Kids need variety to keep their brain and personality developing in a balanced way.

It would be great if a preschooler's day were all fun and games. But most days include a need for discipline of some sort. Authorities abound with conflicting views as to what kind of discipline is best.

I agree with whoever said, *"The best discipline is discipline that works!"* But there are a few basic guidelines that can be followed when disciplining a child.

Above all else, be consistent! Giving in to Johnny's desire to stand on his chair while eating will confuse him when he hears "no" the next time. Consistency goes a long way in keeping peace in the home, and it helps the child develop trust in parents who can be depended on. But "consistent" is probably the hardest thing to be. One day I make up an arbitrary rule like there'll be "no playing with the stereo knobs." Later, I get tired of saying "no" or turning the persistent child's attention elsewhere. So I decide, "What's the big deal about some old stereo knobs?" and there goes my consistency right out the window.

Also, I know a child becomes frustrated if he receives one message from Mother, another from Father. If the messages are frequently inconsistent, the child also learns to manipulate, and play one parent against the other. Therefore, good communication between husband and wife is crucial. It is important for the sitter to know family guidelines and routines as well. Consistency should be maintained in any situation where discipline takes place.

84

Regardless of what discipline is used, preschoolers need to know they are loved and accepted. During this time, most children still have their greatest emotional attachment to the mother, but they are growing more and more independent. They need contacts with friends their age, with other adults, and especially with Father.

Viola told how she helped to draw her husband into the activities of the children. "Before my husband came home from work, I planned special times for the children to be with Daddy. We called it 'taking care of Daddy.' We'd plan to take off his shoes, bring him his slippers; or we'd make something to give him . . . simple things like decorated bookmarks from the corners of envelopes."

What I need is someone to "take care of Mother" too! Sometimes, in order to have the energy and creativity to be actively involved with preschoolers, mothers need to make times to be alone, to get out, to be a little pampered, to ask for help when it's needed. Several couples I know take turns caring for each others' preschoolers. Each couple then has one free evening per month.

And finally, preschool is a good time for a child to start learning about God's love. Preschoolers can't always understand all the words or concepts, but then, who can? Gwen was frustrated about trying to explain who God is to two-and-a-half-year-old Jeffrey. The truth is, as adults we don't fully understand who God is either. We understand parts, and gradually grow in knowledge and depth.

But a preschooler can be told that God is someone very special, more special than anyone in the whole wide world; that God loves him, more than anyone loves him, even more than Mommy and Daddy; and that God wants Jeffrey to love Him too. Putting spiritual truths into words that the child already understands can be stretching and enlightening for parents as well. We begin to understand God's nature and love in fresh, childlike ways.

12

How to Survive
Sunday Morning Hassle

Ever heard of SMH? It's a widespread epidemic, generally affecting women more than men, even in these liberated times (a personal observation). It affects churchgoers 100 percent more often than nonchurchgoers. There is no known cure. But there may be some ways to relieve the symptoms.

To my knowledge, no one has ever given it a name before. But ask almost any parent if they know what "Sunday Morning Hassle" is and they'll probably give a knowing smile—if they don't cry first.

SMH, or Sunday Morning Hassle, is what it takes to get three or more differently paced individuals out the door Sunday morning in such a mood that everyone still feels like worshiping God. It may start with trying to get everyone dressed in halfway coordinated outfits while keeping the baby from falling asleep before leaving for church. It includes wrestling with wiggly little ones in church and shushing outbursts of "Daddy, can I go to the bathroom?" (or worse). It includes the stress Mom feels over the six-month-old not taking her usual morning nap, knowing she will be a bear that afternoon until she has a good nap. It's prying a clingy two-year-old's arms from around one's neck in order to deposit him at the nursery. It's having to chase all over church gathering up books, spilled Cheerios, bottle caps, and Sunday school papers. And last, it's getting home to find a cold oven and an uncooked roast.

No wonder some parents conclude, "It's more trouble than it's worth." And they grant themselves a three-year sabbatical from church.

I was experiencing that same temptation when I started asking other moms and dads if they experience some of the same stress I do each Sunday morning. And I discovered an instant sorority of sorts. Through this sharing, I also began to understand an incident from my childhood that had always stood out in my mind with perplexing clarity.

I grew up in a family with three sisters and one brother. Every Sunday we three girls marched into church with meticulously braided hair. One morning we were running behind as usual. As deacon, my father was in charge of starting the service, and of course, he didn't want to be late. But Mom was struggling to make presentable braids out of our unruly, fly-away hair; our grandmother who lived with us needed to have her hair combed, and our three-week-old baby brother was demanding attention, too. Mom finally just broke down and cried, "Oh, you all just go on and go. I'm staying home." I can't remember whether she went or not, but now I understand as I never could before her rare outburst that memorable Sunday morning.

I have heard of a family who always made it to church on time. They did it by dressing the kids for church before they went to bed Saturday night! That's too drastic for me, but I've found there are some things that can be done the night before in preparation for a smoother Sunday morning.

For our family, Sunday is one time we enjoy a big breakfast together. While many young families opt for cold cereal and juice in order to save time and energy, sometimes I try to conserve morning time by fixing as much of Sunday break-fast as I can the night before. Setting the table, mixing up the pancake batter or scrambled eggs, making the juice, putting the coffee and water in the coffeemaker, getting out necessary pots and pans can save countless steps and distractions in the morning.

I've also started writing the check for the offering the night before and finding the correct offering envelope, which often before had held us up at the last minute.

If one has an infant, bottles can be prepared Saturday evening, and the diaper bag can be packed completely to save that chore in the morning, too.

Jim and Jan are parents of two boys, a two-and-a-half-year-old and a two-month-old. Jan says she starts preparing for Sunday morning on Saturday evening by gathering books, toys, pencils and paper for Marshall, the older boy, to use quietly in church. Another couple, Gene and Gloria, have six- and four-year-old boys. Gloria likes to have all the kids' clothes laid out the night before. Gloria and Jan agree that continuing this head start the next morning is the key to a smoother Sunday.

"I've had to give up trying to sleep in at all," says Gloria. Her husband, Gene, is the pastor of a small, mountain church with about a hundred members, and often he has to take care of last-minute details before worship on Sunday morning. "I don't know why I ever agreed to talk with you about this," Gloria admitted good-naturedly when I called her to get her ideas. "After I hung up from talking to you the other day, I thought, 'Sunday morning is probably our most hectic morning of the week!'"

Jan says that she tries to get showered and dressed as much as possible before the rest of the family is up. Her husband, Jim, fixes breakfast for himself and the older boy, while she nurses the baby. Jim usually teaches Sunday school, so occasionally he has to do some last-minute brushing up. On those days Jan does more. But generally each parent takes care of one child. It takes a team effort to make everything run smoothly on Sunday mornings.

Often a stressful morning at home will carry over to a bad morning at church. Children may internalize the stress at first, but it often comes out later in a difficult goodbye scene with a toddler in the nursery, or perhaps the four-year-old is more fidgety than usual during the worship service.

"I definitely agree that morning stress can carry over to church," Gloria says. At their small church no nursery is provided. "There is a small room with a crib and rocking chair, but it's also a hallway, so it's not the best for sleeping babies." Since Gene is pastor, Gloria keeps both boys with her during worship. There are sometimes as many as fifteen children under the age of five at their church, but because the service tends to be informal, the noises from children are okay.

Most larger churches offer nursery facilities either during Sunday school or worship, or both. But as heavenly as it sounds to sit through worship and Sunday school without squirming little ones, it's certainly not the perfect answer either. Often the nursery attendants can't give the one-on-one care necessary, or it's not quiet enough to put the younger ones to bed for naps. Sometimes inexperienced caretakers don't change diapers often enough, or they might have difficulty keeping the more aggressive children from bugging the smaller ones. And, as one friend of mine admits, her little girl is so active that two consecutive hours in the nursery on Sunday morning—with constant stimulation from all the "different" toys, children, and activities—get her as "high as a kite." Her increased activity then continues well into Sunday afternoon. So it's not as though Sunday Morning Hassle is over as soon as one leaves the kids in the nursery.

If you run into problems of this nature, sometimes it's helpful to open dialogue with the person in charge of the nursery program, the Sunday school superintendent, or the child's teacher. One mother felt that by the time the Sunday school hour rolled around, her toddler was too hungry and too tired to "bother" the Sunday school staff with. So she would take him home to feed and put to sleep. In an open parent-teacher forum, she explained why she was keeping her toddler out of class. Then, a solution seemed obvious to all: begin the educational hour with a snack and a rest time.

Other parents in the forum shared their particular "hassles," and together they arrived at some options to try. I say "try" because everyone knows that what works with one two-year-old won't necessarily do for another.

How to nurse a baby while at church is another Sunday morning issue that may worry the new mother who is breast-feeding. Some feel perfectly comfortable discreetly going about feeding their infants during the worship service, especially on the back benches. But as Jan says, "Murray is such a noisy eater, I don't. I wouldn't be able to concentrate on the service."

At our church we have a half-hour fellowship time between church and Sunday school. Although we left our daughter in the nursery for both services, I usually found a quiet place to nurse her during that break. When our daughter was weaned to the bottle, it was nice for me to let my husband feed her at that time, especially if I was teaching later or if I had business to take care of.

In addition to those issues already mentioned, Sunday morning illness can create another: which parent will stay home to care for a sick child? In this situation, the fact that the mother is breastfeeding an infant or that one parent teaches Sunday school may provide a ready answer. Jan says that although she and Jim share many of the parenting duties, she usually stays home with sick children precisely for those reasons. Or sometimes they all stay home and worship privately. The one time our infant daughter was feeling under the weather on a Sunday morning, my husband enjoyed staying home with her since he sees much less of her during the week than I do because of his long work hours. And for the first time since she was born, I enjoyed going to church without a diaper bag flapping over my shoulder.

Trying to have company for Sunday dinner presents yet another problem in the string of possible Sunday morning hassles. Jan recalls one mini-disaster. "I thought I had everything all organized, and then at the last minute one or two things went wrong so we were late leaving for church. And it wasn't until we were sitting in church that I remembered I hadn't put the chicken and rice in the oven like I had planned." She continues, "We just had our conversation first, rather than after dinner, while we were waiting for the chicken to get done!" She also says they now do more evening entertaining during the week, and she usually fixes simple meals like omelets, toasted cheese sandwiches, or oven dinners for Sunday noon.

Gloria says that she and Gene find it is more convenient for people from their church to come for dinner on Sunday rather than on a weekday. So they have Sunday dinner guests regularly. However, she admits, "I do get kind of hung up on those mornings trying to get dinner ready."

I sometimes make a big dinner of fried chicken and mashed potatoes, and we simply eat at 1:30 or 2:00. I do this mainly because it's one of the most important times for us to enjoy a nice meal together. However, if we do have company on Sunday, it's more often for a casual meal of sandwiches and popcorn in the evening, since our church doesn't have evening services regularly.

Perhaps one bright note to be found in living with Sunday Morning Hassle is the realization that "this too shall pass," and we should be grateful for the blessing of children to our lives. "I think Sunday Morning Hassle affects everybody for a while, going through a period when the children are small when you feel like you want to stay home," Gloria reflected.

We've appreciated immensely the help that other people

have given us at church; people who no longer have such small children but who remember what it was like. They do little things like hold a door open, help us out of the car, hold Michelle while we get our coats on, carry food in for potluck dinners, and take over so we can eat in peace at potlucks. Such thoughtful churchgoers deserve a special place in heaven!

I've also found that it helps to take one Sunday at a time and not assume it's going to be an "Excedrin" day before I even get up. As Gloria says, "Trying to have a smooth Sunday morning is mostly a matter of taking care of small things ahead of time." It is those small things, if not taken care of, that add up to a big hassle.

So what will happen the first Sunday morning you implement a new program of being completely organized? It's possible that some minor catastrophe will occur, like the basement flooding or Billy coming down with the measles. Or maybe it will be like the first Sunday morning we tried our new plan. I felt so organized—clothes were laid out, the coffee was ready to perk, the bottles were ready to go. But we awoke to a slithery, ice-draped world, and church services were canceled all over the county. Had all our preparations been in vain?

No. I felt like a queen in my own castle that morning, as pampered as my eight-month-old daughter. With a minimum of work, breakfast was served, the baby was fed, and we all gathered on the living room floor for some Bible reading and welcome family fellowship.[1]

13

Mom, Billy Called Me Fatso

Most of my fights with my brother and sisters when I was growing up were the normal, "I did not," "You did too," variety. We engaged in name calling and accusations that escalated to a high verbal pitch, but not very often to physical violence. There were fights over whose turn it was to wash dishes or to sit by the window in the car, and others in which we yelled, "Move over to your side of the bed!" Most of these fights we resolved ourselves, which I've now learned is what the experts tell parents too—stay out of a fight unless there's a threat to physical safety or emotional well-being.

But the fight I remember most vividly happened when I was well into adolescence. We lived on a farm and all of us helped with the chores, especially with gathering the 5,000 to 8,000 eggs a day. The work was tedious, but was relieved by good-natured teasing and the small salary we were paid.

One evening I guess I wasn't in the mood for teasing. My sister, who knew she had a particular laugh that really irked me, started laughing at my bad mood. I was usually pretty easygoing, so I think she was as shocked as I was when I shoved a whole case—that's 360 eggs!—at her in the egg storage room.

No matter how much children may love each other, I've yet to find a family that doesn't have occasional misunderstandings, angry words, and hurt feelings.

The scene is too familiar. Billy teases his younger sister; she retaliates by calling him "Fatso"; and soon they are engaged in a who-can-shout-the-worst-name-loudest contest.

If rivalry is as natural and unavoidable as it seems to be, it's helpful to have an understanding of what causes competition between brothers and sisters.

Little children love their parents more than anyone else in the world. Therefore, Danny wants Mom and Dad to love him more than anyone else in the world, including his brother and sister. And he will compete for that love, if he's allowed to. Our task as parents is to squelch the competition as much as possible by letting Danny know that he is special.[1]

It's not easy for parents to explain to children how they love each child differently, but equally. After my oldest sister had her second child, she wrote me, "I used to worry whether I could love a new baby because I loved our little Larry so much. I couldn't imagine sharing that love with another child. But when Bobby came, it wasn't that I was sharing half of Larry's love, but that I had a whole new dose of special love for Bobby." Loving has a way of teaching us to love more.

We can compare this to the way God loves us. He loves each of us equally, but we're each unique, too. When we realize that we are special to God—that he created each of us differently—it helps us treat each other and our children as the special persons they really are!

Another cause for rivalry is the natural urge to be "best" in everything. Part of the hidden anger I held against the sister I threw the eggs at had developed because it seemed she was (is) good at everything—sports, making friends, being popular. Now I console myself that she'd rather go to the dentist than write even a letter, I believe. Children want to excel by bringing home the best report card or by being the kid to score the winning point in the baseball game. As children mature, they can learn that no one person is "best" at everything, and they should be made to feel very good about the things they are good at. Kelly can also learn that bringing home all A's on her report card doesn't mean she is a better person than the child who doesn't.[2]

Competition and fights between brothers and sisters often stem from the feeling that they are being treated unfairly. That doesn't necessarily mean that they *are* treated unfairly. It usually means they have misunderstood, or have been overlooked inadvertently, or a house rule hasn't been fully explained.

"Why do I have to go to bed earlier than my sisters?" Ken asks. "Because I said so" is not a satisfactory answer. It doesn't recognize the feeling that he isn't being treated fairly. Instead, Ken can be told, "You need to go to bed earlier because you're younger, and you need your rest. When you get older, you'll be able to stay up later, too. And remember, I still read *you* a bedtime story. That's a treat your sisters don't get."

Some brothers and sisters fight simply because they have been together too much. This happens especially during summer months, on weekends, and on vacations from school. Think about it! Young children who eat, play, work, sleep, and travel together may have more contact with each other than a married couple has.[3] And like adults, they get tired of each other. Parents can help avoid these kinds of arguments by trying to find ways to let each child be by himself—by encouraging individual bike rides or walks, by suggesting play in separate rooms, or by giving different jobs to each.

Carole and Andrew Calladine have four boys ranging in

age from five to fourteen. Carole and Andrew knew that all siblings fight, but they wondered if the fighting had to go to the extremes that their boys went to. They didn't want their sons to grow up hating each other.

One thing the Calladines discovered is that parents often unwittingly turn their children into competitors for attention.[4] For instance, parents often ignore kids *except* when they're fighting and, in this way, encourage them to argue. Children may even compare themselves to siblings and try to get more parental attention and affection by making loud claims like, "I'm fastest," or "smartest," or "best" in any number of ways. In addition, as parents, we have probably all been guilty of saying things like, "Karen, why don't you play quietly like Dottie does?" and of making other verbal comparisons. It is important that instead of being treated as competitors, children are treated as equals, each accepted and loved for himself.

The Calladines also feel it works best to intervene in sibling conflicts in only two circumstances: if there is physical abuse, or if the noise level is more than they, the parents, can take. If a child is losing his temper and physically abusing a brother or sister, they send both to separate corners of a room to cool off. A work assignment is sometimes given to each, which does at least two things: it helps burn up some of that excess energy, and also helps the child feel better about him or herself. (After all, a child must be at least a little bit good if he does a good deed.) After the cooling down process, a mediator should help the children discuss their differences.

Suppose two children enter the kitchen. The older one has a basketball under his arm. Pointing at his younger brother, he says, "Mom, get this brat out of the driveway."

The younger child shouts back, "Well, it's not your driveway any more than it is mine."

"I was there first, playing basketball."

"So, I want to ride my fire engine. It's my house, too."

Finally, the parent intervenes and says, "Guess you two have a problem. You both want to use the driveway. How are you going to work it out?"

A discussion follows as the two squabblers talk through their roles, their rights, and their problem. The parent stays out of the discussion but *doesn't* leave the room. She acts as a stabilizer and mediator by stating the problem and listing the solutions that the brothers propose. The two finally reach a compromise: the fireman will have the driveway for twenty minutes, then it becomes a basketball court until dinner.[5] The boys set the kitchen timer. Both children feel it's a fair trade-off—the one who gets to use the driveway first compromised a shorter playing time. Whether or not the arrangement *is* fair, the important thing is that both *feel* it's fair.

As parent and mediator you should help your children find the right time and place to discuss their differences. They should be taught that it's important to do their confronting in private, not in front of brothers or sisters or friends. Children get embarrassed, just like adults.

They should also be taught the difference between fighting just to hurt each other, and fighting in order to settle an issue. Help a child state how *she* is feeling in "I" language. When younger Willie gets into older Karen's coloring set, she should say, "I feel mad when you get into my things," rather than, "You baby! You always ruin my things."

Sometimes it's hard to determine "who started it" when teasing happens. When Carole and Andrew's two oldest children were five years old and seven months old, the family enjoyed a beautiful day of picnicking with a friend. There had been no fights and no squalls from the baby. But just as they got ready to leave, the baby started crying loudly for what seemed to be no reason at all. Finally, they told the little one, "If you don't stop crying, you will be put right to bed when we get home without your song and storytime in the rocker." The howls quieted. Then on the way home the crying erupted again. The parents were only too glad to deposit him in his room for his nap, *without* the song and story in the rocker, just as they had threatened. They praised the older child for being so good on the picnic and told him he could go out and play with his friend. He left, happy and humming.

It was only then that their friend stepped in. "I don't want to interfere . . . but . . . it was the five-year-old who had been teasing. He'd offer a pretty little pebble to the baby, and then jerk it away just as baby's hand would reach out." Of course, the five-year-old's hand was safely hiding in his pocket by the time the parents turned around.[6] As so often happens, the parents had unwittingly punished the wrong child! In this case, the "punished" child was so young that a verbal apology would have been useless. But generally, it's very important for parents to admit when a mistake has been made, then follow up with an appropriate punishment for the right child.

It's tough to come home after a day of office infighting or a misunderstanding with a factory supervisor to be faced with more of the same. So when both parents work outside the home, special instructions should be given to have the babysitter or after-school care-giver follow parents' patterns for settling squabbles before the parents arrive. This can get sticky, because it's not always possible or desirable to change care-givers just because they have different approaches to discipline or settling arguments.

If both parents are away for part of the child's day at home, it takes extra effort to keep communication lines open, to make sure expectations are clear—in short, to do all of the things that conflict-resolution experts suggest. That's a tall order, and there will be plenty of failures. We can only pray and trust God that our children will thrive in spite of our inadequacies.

Measles, Mumps, and I-Hate-School Stomachaches

When I was a little girl, Mom had a beautiful, tiny china tea set that she'd bring out for me to play with only when I was sick. The rest of the year, it stayed in its box on a shelf in her closet—I can still picture where.

Another mother told me when her children are ill she brings out the family photo album and her jewelry chest— the kids are entertained for hours.

Whether it's measles, mumps, or just a plain "I-hate-school" stomachache, illness in the family presents a time of special challenge to parents. During these times, you will need extra energy, patience, creativity to think of things to do, as well as sheer stamina. In fact, I've given up trying to get anything done when a child is sick. And it's not only the sick child who has special requirements in extended illnesses, the parents and other children may experience crises as well.

But let's start by looking at some problems associated with a minor illness. It's a familiar scene. Tommy comes into the kitchen looking a little flush and croaks, "I have a sore throat, Mom." Mom takes his temperature, gets the aspirin and the fruit juice, and thinks, "Is he too sick to stay with the sitter?

Should I take a day of vacation to stay home?" After breakfast, Mom decides to stay home, then wonders whether or not to call the doctor.

Especially if both parents work, just caring for the ill child's physical needs presents a problem. Which parent is most able to stay home from his or her job for a day? Perhaps this will depend on current job loads or on the type of work each does. Could Dad do some of his work at home?

However, if both parents must go to work, a second option is to have someone come in, perhaps a friendly and familiar neighbor or a regular babysitter. *Lucky* is the child whose grandmother or grandfather lives close by and is willing to stay with him.

A third option is to send the child to his regular day-care center. This at first may seem heartless, but for the family with two working parents it may be necessary. In fact, many parents choose their day-care facilities on the basis of the arrangements it offers for children who are ill.

Older children can be left alone at home, *if* they are comfortable with that, and *if* a parent is immediately available by telephone. Some children like the independence that staying alone implies. Of course, this option should be chosen only in situations where the child is not seriously ill, and when parents feel it is a safe choice.

Depending on the specific circumstances and the contagiousness of the illness, some working parents might consider the possibility of taking their child who is not feeling well along with them to work. If this is the case, check with your employer and fellow workers first to make sure they don't mind.

When a child needs to be hospitalized for a more serious illness, it's important to know that children vary in their reaction to hospitalization, just like adults do. Some look forward to it, almost like a special treat. Other children are almost overcome with hysterical fears of being rejected or left forever at the hospital. They may even fear they'll die like Grandma did if they stay in the hospital.

An operation is basically an injury. And if a child is not properly prepared for it, he may feel his parents and his doctor cooperated in a giant conspiracy to make him hurt a lot. For instance, Amy probably feels just fine as she enters the hospital for a tonsillectomy. After the operation, she wonders why she feels so badly when she has been told that her hospital visit will make her feel better. Then she is comforted as she remembers the doctor told her that her throat would feel really bad right after the operation, but that it would soon start to feel better.

This need for honesty with children about what they can expect when they go to the doctor or the hospital surfaced again and again as I read articles and books describing how to help children with sickness. Children feel betrayed if they are not dealt with honestly. For instance, if I tell Michelle a shot is not going to hurt, when it does hurt, she feels I've lied to her, which I have.

A woman who is director of a hospital's special youth program shares the following examples of this type of betrayal:

- A twelve-year-old boy said, "I was lying on the x-ray table getting a blood test." The doctor couldn't find the vein. "He promised that he would stop when it started hurting me. He didn't stop at all. That made me start crying even more."
- A seven-year-old who was in the hospital for a series of blood tests confided that since he wasn't very sick, the doctors had decided to give his blood away to other, very sick patients.
- A six-year-old thought dirty dish water was traveling through the intravenous apparatus hooked up to him. [1]

You can avoid these kinds of misconceptions by explaining to your child what will happen in the hospital honestly and in terms he can understand.

In addition, a child shouldn't be told not to cry. Often we may be tempted to repeat lines from our own childhood, like "only babies cry" or even worse, "boys don't cry." The truth is, we don't want to hear the ailing child cry. Crying is not easy to listen to. It hurts us, too. We're proud when we can go home and report, "Johnny didn't even cry when he got his shot." But we fail to recognize that he may have needed to cry very much. If we can begin to view crying as the healthy outlet that it is, then some of the pain that we, as parents, feel will be relieved.

The strain that having a seriously ill child can put on a marriage is yet another problem. Many times couples who related very well before their child became sick lapse into miscommunication when faced with the trauma of illness.

Bill and Ginny had a good marriage. Then, when their only child was still an infant, he was found to have cystic fibrosis. Ginny was determined to protect her child in every way, and she insisted on carrying out the time-consuming treatments at home all by herself. In addition to her regular work of caring for the home, she was literally Eric's nurse day and night.

As you can imagine, Ginny was soon exhausted, completely absorbed in her son's needs and condition. In her busyness she didn't notice Bill's unhappiness. Bill resented the care she was giving to their child. But he was ashamed of his feelings, so he didn't want to express that resentment to his wife.

Eventually Bill became so unhappy he thought his only solution was to escape from the marriage and he asked for a separation. However, Ginny persuaded him to go for marriage counseling before they did that. Happily, through several months of counseling, they were able to renew their commitment to their marriage.[2]

This is a normal response to serious illness in a child. The fear of losing a child often causes initial alienation from a spouse. It's also natural to feel a certain amount of anger and guilt. Why us? What did I do to cause the illness? Or what did my partner do to cause the illness? It's difficult not to blame the parent on whose side the gene was carried, especially if the disease is inherited.

Each parent reacts to the grief and worry in different ways. A pediatrician writes that one spouse, perhaps the wife, may seek comfort and close physical contact with her husband, while he may tend to retreat and become silent and aloof instead of drawing closer. Burdened by the extra expense of the illness, the husband may try to bury his pain under more and more work to help in any way he can with the expense. The wife interprets this as: "He doesn't care about us and spends more and more time at his job."[3]

All of these stresses can contribute to a real strain on the marriage. Partners need to open up their feelings about the crisis they are experiencing. Sometimes a helper—a professional counselor, relative, pastor, or trusted friend—is needed to comfort and advise a couple as they struggle through such difficult times.

God has promised to be with us in our pain—and that means his care upholds parents as well as their sick child.

Although illness is trying and saddening, especially for children, let's think for a minute what strengths we can help them gain from the experience.

A child can learn empathy for friends who are ill. Or perhaps he can increase his understanding of a grandparent who frequently complains about this ache or that pain.

A sick youngster can gain a new appreciation for life, for good health, and for the intricate way our bodies are made. Use the opportunity of healing to explain how God made our bodies with the equipment to fight off a germ, to replace blood, and to mend a broken bone. It is the perfect time to teach your child how God lovingly guides us through the valley of illness.

Most importantly, a child can learn that through prayer we should *continually* turn to God for health and life itself, not *only* when we are sick or in trouble.

However, if a child is seriously ill, parents may find themselves *unable* to pray—questioning God and unable to communicate. This tendency to question one's faith is normal—and parents needn't feel guilty about it. Well-meaning comforters may come with advice like, "If your faith was just stronger, Tommy would get well." But families who have been through crises say that friends who let you cry, let you express anger and fear and doubt are the most helpful.

Friends who translate their faith in God into loving action—such as sitting with family members through long waits in the hospital; transportation to and from a distant hospital; meals brought in; laundry taken care of; babysitting; money gifts to help with expenses—are lifesavers. It may be that later, after the crisis has passed, memories of these tangible expressions of love will minister to the ones who temporarily lost their confidence in God. For instance, Bob and Ann may say something like, "We asked where God was when our son died. Now we know God was there all the time, through the love and support of people from the church."

Times of minor illness can become experiences children will look back on later, with real fondness and love, as times of positive learning. That may sound far-fetched, particularly if you have ever been cooped up with three active children who are just-about-but-not-quite-over the chicken pox. And with a more serious illness, it may even seem impossible.

But a TV news-magazine show I saw helped me realize how growth and learning is possible even in a serious illness. A young boy who had been ill and weak with brain cancer for months was interviewed. He talked about how depressed and full of self-pity he had been. With the help of a doctor, he was able to "pinpoint his problem" of self-pity, as he stated, very adult-like. He was put in touch with another boy, clear across the country, who had just been diagnosed as having bone cancer and had had his leg amputated at the knee. Through long-distance telephone calls, the boys helped each other to new understanding and camaraderie. Their conversations ranged from sharing their latest knock-knock joke, to discussing the fears they felt when undergoing chemotherapy. As one of the boys put it, "When Paul says he knows how I feel, I know he really means it."

These boys may not have been healed physically, but at least they were healed emotionally—relating in a wholesome manner. And that's probably the key to coping with any illness—finding ways to stay "on top of it" emotionally.

But Doctor,
How Much "Hyper" Is Normal?

I remember so well the first night I began to wonder if our daughter was hyperactive. It had been a Sunday full of the usual hecticness—to church without a morning nap, to a potluck lunch with lots of kids jockeying to play with Michelle, and finally home to a late afternoon nap. With supper I fed Michelle a lot of leftover jello from the potluck which, to a seven month old, was a delicacy in her new-found world of solid foods.

That night we had guests over, and after several futile attempts at putting Michelle to bed, I gave in and let her stay up until they left. She was obviously tired but couldn't sleep. Her little arms and legs thrust about frantically, fighting my grip as I rocked her. Then I remembered the jello and all the sweetened tea she had had at the potluck, and began to panic. What if she's supersensitive to sugar and hyperactive?

Now I know better. Michelle was overtired, overstimulated, and not sleepy because of her late nap. She was also responding to a very frustrated momma. The extra sugar probably had something to do with her high energy level, since her diet normally has very little sugar in it. But overall, her patterns of behavior are calm, easygoing, happy. Since that evening, I've also learned that true hyperactivity doesn't really become obvious in children until later in the preschool years and for some unknown reason, it affects boys 80 percent more often than girls. (Therefore, in this chapter I use male pronouns to refer to the hyperactive child.)

So why include this chapter on a subject with which (thankfully) I have no firsthand experience as yet? Simply for this reason: I think most parents wonder from time to time (as we did), "Is our child hyperactive, or is this normal behavior that will pass?" With the increased additives in our diets and the highly sugared drinks, cereals, and snacks that are so heavily advertised and consumed by a whole nation of youngsters, more and more parents will probably be facing the frustration of dealing with hyperactivity. Also, many of us know friends or relatives with a hyperactive child.

Just as I mistakenly labeled my child that night, many people toss around the term "hyperactive" to describe any overactive, mischievous, or boisterous child. But misusing the term is a disservice to the approximate 6 to 10 percent of grade school children who struggle with medically diagnosed "hyperkinesis," the illness more commonly known as "hyperactivity."

What exactly is hyperactivity? Although health care professionals find it difficult to clearly define, there are some typical behavior patterns associated with the hyperactive child that all parents should be aware of.

- *Clumsy.* The child is not only overactive, but much of his activity is without direction or purpose.
- *Destructive.* He intentionally damages toys and other property.
- *Forgetful.* He lives for the present and doesn't remember the consequences of previous misbehavior.
- *Restless.* He constantly fidgets, talks, and touches excessively.

- *Non-studious.* At school, he often makes disruptive noises, leaves his seat, and has a short attention span.
- *Alienated.* Often his peers do not accept him and will not play with him.

These adjectives could describe any normally high-strung child. Because hyperactivity is so hard to definitely diagnose, sometimes it's difficult to find help. And to confuse things even more, doctors and researchers now recognize that a child may be mildly, moderately, or severely hyperactive. But just because a child doesn't erupt in frequent screaming tantrums, it doesn't mean that he isn't suffering from other behavioral problems and that he can't or shouldn't be helped by some kind of therapy.

The problems of caring for a hyperactive child are only more complicated if both parents work and someone else provides care for part or all of a day. Parents in this situation constantly struggle with questions that are difficult to answer—Who can I hire to give loving care to a child who needs lots of attention and activity, and who seems to push everyone's patience to its limit? What caregiver wants the added hassle? What if my child must follow a limited, specialized diet? Dare I ask the babysitter's other children to go without candy just because I don't want my children eating much of it? Can hyperactivity really be managed?

Although parents may not find easy, clear-cut answers to their questions, they can help the hyperactive child by keeping informed about the problem and remaining sensitive to the child's special needs.

A hyperactive child experiences many negative reactions to his behavior. He may find it difficult to make and keep friends because he won't share toys or because he can't play at one game for a long period of time. At home, brothers and sisters may find it difficult to like him. Unfortunately, these negative reactions increase his feelings of "I'm different. I'm no good. I can't do anything right." It is not surprising that one of the hyperactive child's key problems is low self-esteem.

It's a continual, self-defeating cycle. Billy wants to be liked by the other children, so he tries to win their affection by clowning, showing off, or by picking on others. This behavior, of course, doesn't succeed in winning any friends, and he's smart enough to realize the other kids don't like him. His self-esteem sinks even lower.

One way for parents to help is to change their own image of the child. That is, rather than seeing a restless, frantic bundle of disaster, envision a child that is calmly in control of his actions. When the child misbehaves, focus on the behavior, not on the child. For instance, instead of yelling, "Don't be so careless—you're always breaking something," say, "I get angry when my special treasures get broken." Such a message implies, "I love you, but I don't like having special things broken."

Sue, a nurse and mother of four, met me for lunch to talk about her experience of living with a hyperactive child. She and her family have been on a twelve-year search to find an adequate diagnosis of their son Ronnie's problem. Meanwhile they have lived with the tantrums, the constant fidgeting and restless activity, and the frustrating waits to find help.

"No doctor has ever agreed with our conclusion that Ronnie is hyperactive," were her first words after dispensing with polite table talk. "But I first felt he was different when he started to walk. I literally couldn't let him out of my sight for more than a minute or two at a time."

When Ronnie was a toddler, if Sue took her eyes off him for just a short time while working outside, he was gone. And she didn't know in which direction to begin looking. Well-meaning friends told her, "Oh, you were just used to raising girls. He's just a normal, active boy." But Sue felt it was more than that. When she took him to the doctor, he was quiet and reserved, so it was difficult for the doctor to diagnose hyperactivity. Not wanting to hear the worst anyway, she accepted the doctor's diagnosis, "He is a bit highly charged—but just cope the best you can."

One reason doctors may be slow to diagnose a child as truly hyperactive is because of the damaging nature of such labels. But as one child specialist says, to refuse to diagnose and treat a child for abnormal behavior just because labels have been misused is not the answer either. He says, after twenty-five years of clinical experience, he finds he can't "dismiss as myth a set of problems repeatedly brought to [him] by distressed and overwhelmed parents."[1]

It wasn't until Ronnie went to grade school—where *other* adults spent extended periods of time with him—that Sue sought further help. Teachers began reporting the typical hyperactive behavior: a short attention span, being easily distracted by every little noise made in the classroom, and a tendency to show off and clown around excessively. Ronnie also seemed to have a mild learning disability, which is often the case with a hyperactive child. Although the hyperactive child is usually of average to above average intelligence, learning disabilities often mar his ability to find success in the average classroom. For this reason, it is often helpful for the hyperactive child to go to a resource teacher for one or several periods of the day. In Ronnie's case, he behaved and learned exceptionally well with the resource teacher, but seemed to fall apart in the distracting atmosphere of a larger classroom.

As the hyperactive child gets older, he realizes how he'd like to be, but still has great difficulty reaching his goal. And so parents, child, and brothers and sisters have tough going as the struggle to manage hyperactivity continues.

"There's not a whole lot that outsiders can do," Sue responded when I asked her how friends and relatives can be of help. "But it would help if I felt that people weren't being so critical. I feel like people think we aren't disciplining our child."

Grandparents may be especially critical. Grandpa may say, "*My* dad never called it hyperactivity; he just called it *spoiled* and our treatment was a sound spanking!"

There are several reasons Grandpa may never have heard of hyperactivity. One, less was known about it when he was young, just as less was known about cancer and diabetes. Two, people were more private about their family problems then. They seldom spoke about them with friends and seeking counseling was practically unheard of. Three, there are certainly more artificial substances and additives in our lives now than fifty to seventy-five years ago. So, it's really unfair of him to dismiss hyperactivity as a product of permissive parents.

Where does that leave outsiders? How can family and friends respond? Sue says, "Just try to understand these children." If you know your child is in a classroom with a hyperactive child, help him understand why it's especially cruel to pick on and bug a hyperactive child.

Sue remembered a time she went on a field trip with her son's school class. She carefully observed her son. Ronnie *tried* to be good, but the other kids knew, from past experience, that they could get a "rise" out of him if they picked on him. Eventually the constant teasing and picking and prodding became so irritating that he couldn't contain himself anymore. The teacher saw only his explosion and not the continual picking that preceded his outburst. Children don't tease to be intentionally cruel; they do it because it seems *fun*. Adults generally (!) know when it's time to stop teasing, but children don't have that kind of mature judgment. So it's up to teachers and parents to observe behavior as closely as they can, to make sure they see the real reasons behind Ronnie's explosions.

When I left Sue, she was hopeful about an upcoming appointment with yet another counselor, and living meanwhile with the tantrums. She holds her breath when Ronnie comes home from school each night, for she is never quite sure what his mood will be. However, she does find some relief in working part of the day outside the home.

She also expressed comfort in the fact that God gives her strength and the courage to keep trying and hoping. And she admitted that Ronnie, like many other hyperactive youngsters, is a warm and sensitive child emitting a special kind of charm. Yet she was clearly troubled, worried that her child would become so alienated and unable to communicate that helping him would be even more difficult. She was worried that time was running out.

"No one can make it easy to raise a hyperactive child," says a medical social worker.[2] But here are some suggestions for dealing with a hyperactive child that are also good common sense for parenting any child.

When giving instructions, make sure the child understands the instructions so he can fulfill expectations. Sometimes parents rattle off a whole list of things to do, forgetting that children forget easily and are distracted by other things. This is especially true for the hyperactive child. It is easier for him to understand simple directions like, "It's time to take your bath," rather than a long, rational explanation about the importance of personal hygiene!

To help him focus his activity, let the hyperactive child participate in deciding what chores need to be done and how he will accomplish them. For instance, it is probably too much to expect a hyperactive child to make his bed, wash and dress, eat breakfast, gather schoolbooks, and feed the dog before going to school in the morning. So suggest options that divide the chores into manageable groups that can easily be completed and let the child choose when he wants to do them. (Maybe he could make his bed and feed the dog as soon as he gets home from school in the afternoon, then lay out his clothes and books at night.) If parents establish regular, predictable routines for the hyperactive child, it helps him avoid wasted motion in frenzied activity.[3]

Much has been made of recent studies linking hyperactivity with food additives, preservatives, artificial flavorings, and sugar. When reading supermarket labels, it seems that just about everything has some kind of additive. A diet eliminating all of the offending foods is very difficult to follow. But I think the diet approach is at least worth trying. There are a number of good books outlining acceptable diets for the hyperactive child. If the whole family does without the offending foods, the child won't feel so cheated by being denied ice cream and other treats. One way to encourage diet modification is to offer to buy non-food treats, like amusement park tickets, a new toy, or a game, with the money saved by not buying candy, desserts, and sugar-coated cereals.

Beyond the daily coping, parents of hyperactive children also grapple with larger questions—How can we help our child secure success in a "normal" world? How can we maintain a sense of stability and wholeness? How are our other children affected? What about the stress on our marriage?[4]

Having a few minutes alone or even a weekend away from the children can help give new perspective to the problems. One mother called dealing with hyperactivity a roller coaster of progress and regression. She said the coming of spring and Easter each year was a reminder of "the *hope* of resurrection and renewal" for her family.[5]

Taming the One-Eyed Monster

For about four years, I circuited church and community groups telling parents "how to tame the one-eyed monster in the living room."

Then I quit, partly because my job and interests had moved on to other things, but also partly because I no longer had the answers. In short, I became a parent. Funny how people without kids so often seem to have all the answers for those who do.

Oh sure, I always apologized to audiences, saying that *they* were really the experts on the use of TV in the home, and I invited their ideas and responses. But it wasn't until my own daughter was about fifteen months old and was begging to see "Ernie-Bert" at ten o'clock in the morning that I began to realize how inadequate scholarly studies on television viewing were when applied to *my* living room. How do you explain to a fifteen-month-old that Ernie and Bert (characters from public broadcasting's "Sesame Street") aren't on TV right now and furthermore it's not good to watch TV all day? For that moment, an explanation that "Ernie and Bert went bye-bye" was sufficient, but I knew that all too soon that wouldn't be a satisfactory answer for all requests to watch TV.

When Michelle was twenty months old, I found it both interesting and alarming to see how much she was absorbing. When the football players fell down in a heap, she said, "Fall down, ouchie boom!" and then followed by falling down herself. Her behavior told me that she knew that people ordinarily get hurt when they fall down, but did she understand why those people on the TV screen were doing it? She mimicked the commercial for "Chlor-*ah*-septic," lit up when anyone mentioned "McDonald's," and danced in response to rhythmic music. So when her father and I watched a movie or show with any shooting or violence in it, I wondered increasingly how much she understood.

In spite of the fact that I'm no longer so free in handing out advice about how to use TV creatively, I'm more *concerned* than *ever* about that monster in my living room.

The average North American spends at least three to four hours watching TV every day.[1] In just twenty-five years TV has gone from being a novelty, a plaything for the rich and the inventors, to being one of the most common pieces of household furniture. For instance, how many people do we know who *don't* have TV? And how many do we know who have two or more sets?

In terms of history, it is such a recent phenomenon that only in the last ten to fifteen years have researchers begun to study the effects of TV on our lifestyles, values, and decisions. But now that we're aware of the problems, what do we do? Do we label each TV set sold with a caution that "watching TV may be hazardous to your health"? Or more extremely, do we place the TV set out with the trash to be hauled away?

One family who decided to make the TV unavailable for just one week said, "It was amazing how few arguments there were . . . about programs, homework, or music practicing . . . how much better we all slept, and most important of all, how little we missed."[2]

Other families who've "kicked the TV habit" say they read more, listen to good music, play cards, entertain more, and spend more time just talking. But banning it from the home is not the *only* solution to using TV in a wise, healthy, upbuilding manner. There are other alternatives.

There are a number of good reasons to watch TV! After a day of hard physical labor, or taxing mental work, it's refreshing to relax with a good comedy or an involving drama. TV has opened up our world; we now think in terms of global community, or worldwide neighbors, instead of just a small neighborhood. And certainly there are moving moments on TV—when I feel a lump rising in my throat as I watch a husband and wife reconcile a marriage, or when I am inspired by a feature about a person who has overcome a disability.

A first step in using TV wisely is deciding to watch specific programs. Use guides to select which programs may be worthwhile.

Another thing to do is evaluate why *you* watch television. Is it an escape from other tasks? Is it escape from involvement with children or spouse? Do you watch for rest and relaxation? Are there television programs you schedule your life around?

Some people automatically turn on their TV sets when they get up in the morning or enter their home in the evening. And we all know of people who have become so involved with the soap operas that their conversation centers on the problems of the sudsy heroines.

Keep in mind that children first learn discriminatory viewing from their parents. If Dad and Mom plop themselves in front of the TV set for hours on end, it's not a very good example of creativity for the children.

A third step in using TV more wisely is to watch TV programs with the children. Most experts warn heavily against using TV as a babysitter for the young child. Working parents may want to choose child care partly on the basis of how much TV viewing is allowed at the day-care center or sitter's home. It's a real temptation to grab a few minutes for myself when I get home from work and Michelle is absorbed in her love affair with Mister Rogers and Mr. McFeely. I too succumb and use TV as a sitter sometimes. But I've found that Michelle picks up even more new words and concepts when I watch Mister Rogers with her and verbalize for her what we are seeing.

As you watch TV, with older children especially, look for TV characters who care about others. Look for women who are competent in a variety of jobs, or for fathers in roles that are dignified and respected. Comment on them. Look for people from different cultural and ethnic backgrounds. When kids learn to think about what they are seeing and hearing on TV, it's more likely that when they're watching on their own, they will do some thinking instead of just passively watching.

After a program is over, *talk* about it. Talk about ways that TV characters could solve their problems without using violence, or about how violence hurts people. The aftereffects of violence are rarely shown on TV. Parents can also raise questions about advertisements and how certain foods can cause cavities, or about toys that don't work like the commercial says.

TV really is a "window on the world." What we see through that window—especially about people with whom we do not come in contact in actual life—forms many of our impressions or opinions about them. For instance, from the picture presented on TV, what is a likely impression of American Indians? Or of Asian-Americans? Of women? Of teenagers? Of politicians?

Television uses stereotypes of certain people because it is a simple way to present an image or idea that is easily identifiable. It saves time in establishing character or defining plot, and makes it easier to achieve humor. Producers also know that certain stock characters (such as the good, white male cop) are favorably received and get higher ratings.[3]

Specifically, men are often cast as incompetent in the kitchen; in family relationships, they are often demanding and unable to express affection. Women are shown as sex objects, dying to get married, or as "superwomen" who achieve it all. Minorities are often assigned the "bad guy roles"—the hit men. Children are shown as cute afterthoughts, or pesky, stubborn adolescents. Older people are often shown as victims of crime, senile, or non-productive to society. Certainly ministers and priests are frequently stereotyped as bungling and ineffective.

On the other hand, we do have positive examples on TV of women as competent managers, and blacks as highly skilled doctors or cops. But many of the daytime reruns persist in perpetuating old stereotypes.

By the time most kids graduate from high school, they will have seen over three hundred and fifty thousand TV commercials.[4] That's about one-third of a million!

Advertisements are essential to commercial TV as we know it. They provide us with needed information about products and services available in the community. There are many commercials that are delightfully produced; some are thoughtful, touching, veritable pieces of art.

But seeing commercial upon commercial—being begged, cajoled, threatened, and told to buy this, eat that, go here, wear this—results in people buying items they don't really need for needs they never knew they had! Commercials such as those that promise lasting happiness as a result of using the right toothpaste play to our basic needs for love and security.

How do I as a Christian respond to Christ's words, "Do not worry about what you will wear and eat. Look at the sparrows and lilies of the field. They do not toil, neither do they spin. Yet Solomon in all his glory was not clothed like one of these. Surely, your heavenly Father cares for *you!*"[5]

The clothing of simplicity—of beauty without having to buy the latest beauty cream, of being happy just having family and friends around, of keeping and repairing the objects we already have—this we can keep in mind as we view commercials. Happiness is *not* the latest model car sitting in our driveway! Life is not measured by status symbols.

On the positive side, there are frequent news specials and documentary features that are well done, timely, and thoroughly researched. The problem is that unless a feature also "entertains" in a sensational way, the program simply is not watched by many and gets low ratings. Then stations or networks become more reluctant to schedule these informative programs. When a half a rating point means thousands and even millions of advertising dollars, we can understand why networks are cautious about scheduling too many programs that attract fewer viewers.

It's important for viewers to write and let stations know when they've appreciated a particular program, especially a documentary or special program that may not have received the highest ratings.

Many have found out that yes, it is possible to effect change. After all, the airwaves belong to us, the citizens. There exists a certain mystique about people who run TV stations and produce programs. They are celebrities. And we tend to forget they are also real people. Some are parents of children who are concerned about the TV programs their children watch. So, letters to the *people* at TV stations can have an impact on future programing.

When a program is violent, distasteful, or obnoxious, write a thoughtful, direct letter to the general manager of the station. (Try to find out his or her name before writing.) Addressing just one concern per letter is more helpful than piling a barrage of complaints into a single letter.

Another effective way to bring about change in TV programing is to monitor and keep records of which sponsors advertise on which shows. Then, write letters to the sponsors stating your views on the program. If a significant number of people object to certain programs, the sponsors of that show may reconsider their advertising policies. Or if the viewer response is very positive, they may choose to risk advertising again on a very good program which may have had a lower rating.

TV is here to stay, and if anything, will probably become even a more pervasive and dominant force in our society. Video games, working from computer terminals in the home, cable, pay TV, and home satellite dishes are commonplace. We're becoming increasingly technologically sophisticated (spit that out without tongue twisting!). In spite of sophistication, controlling TV in our homes can be as simple as turning the off button on our set, and as complex as answering a ten-year-old's question, "But if you don't want me to see so many commercials, why don't you get us 'Home Box Office' movies?" I certainly don't have as many answers as I used to. But I do know that practicing being a critical viewer has helped me be more aware of what I'm watching, and has motivated me to turn the TV off more often!

17

How to Take the $ Out of Chritma and Put Christ Back In

In spite of the too-busy feeling that often accompanies Christmas, most of us love the planning of secret surprises, the anticipation of family gatherings, the beauty of once-a-year adornments for the home. That is, we enjoy these when we're not feeling too scroogish, or too busy from trying to hold down jobs and still keep up with hectic schedules.

The Advent season is one of waiting, of promise, of watching expectantly with renewed hope for Christ's coming. We watch for some new insight or tingly feel-good-all-over instant.

Too often, however, after Christmas we get that let-down feeling—after-Christmas blues or depression. Perhaps that could be avoided if we set our hopes on the right things to begin with. If we expect to receive complete pleasure from the giving and receiving of gifts, from the making and taking of food, then, indeed, we will be left with an empty feeling after the holidays. But if we set our hopes on experiencing the reality of God in a new way, we will not be disappointed.

The example of the Hebrew prophet and prophetess, Sim-

121

eon and Anna, illustrates what I mean. They watched and waited for the Christ child for many years. And, they were rewarded with Christ's presentation in the temple at the time he was eight days old. Immediately they knew that he was the One they had been waiting for—unlike the innkeeper, or the thousands of others who had not watched expectantly and who missed the privilege of knowing and seeing Christ.

In the same way, we will be rewarded with a new sense of what Christ's coming meant to the world if we do not allow ourselves to become swept away with the tide of tinsel, gifts, and parties.

A little boy, anxious for Christmas, kept quizzing his mother about the number of gifts he was getting. Exasperated, not only with his questions, but also with the values he was expressing, she told him that it wasn't important how many gifts one was *getting,* but how many gifts one was *giving.* After a few minutes of thoughtful silence, the little boy asked, "Well, Mommy, how many gifts are you giving me then?"

Sometimes we're just as slow to catch on to the real meaning of our Christmas celebrations. And sometimes we're just as selfish, whether in innocence or full knowledge. But if we can work our way through the layers of wrappings to experience a fresh coming of Christ into our lives, then we will truly know the joy of Christmas.

One way to maximize the true meaning of Christmas is to focus on a celebration that values people over things. To me this is the biblical approach, as set forth in Christ's Sermon on the Mount. "Do not store up for yourselves treasures on earth, . . . but treasures in heaven . . ." (Matt. 6:19–20, NIV). "But seek first his kingdom and his righteousness, and all these things will be given to you as well" (Matt. 6:33, NIV).

That means if you need to make a choice between visiting a friend in the hospital or baking that extra batch of cookies, you may choose the visit. Or if it's a choice between playing with the kids and wrapping gifts, you may choose to let the kids help and be content with less-than-perfectly wrapped gifts.

For most of us, gift-giving is an integral part of Christmas. Some families decide together to pool the money they would have spent on unneeded gifts for each other and give it to some charity or mission project. And while that's a commendable solution for those who choose it, there are many valid reasons for giving gifts to each other at Christmas as well. When family members are scattered across the country and it's impossible to get together every year, then gifts can serve the valuable function of linking family members. Gifts serve as tokens of love.

For that reason, gifts that we make with our hands often mean more than those purchased with money. However, for those who work full-time, it can still be meaningful to give gifts bought with money because money is time invested; money represents our time, unique skills, and love. So we don't need to feel guilty if we don't have time to make all the gifts we'd like to make! In fact, purchasing a gift rather than making it can allow us to spend more time with family, which in turn, can be another demonstration of valuing people over things.

Some homemade gifts can be given throughout the whole year to save time at Christmas. Each year I struggle over what to give to my grandmother. Grandma has all the bottles of lotion, sachet, and hankies she could possibly need. She has no need for a Cuisinart or Hotdogger. Her eyesight isn't good, so she can't do much reading. The sewing box, clock radio, and lamp ideas have all been exhausted long ago.

Since I live six-hundred miles away, I can't offer to drive her to town or to the doctor, or invite her over for meals. But I know my grandma is lonely. Finally, one year I thought of promising to write her a letter once a month. To remind myself of these "letter writing appointments," I wrote a note on my calendar and made sure it didn't get overlooked.

Another idea for an elderly friend, a shut-in, or someone who finds herself in the hospital at Christmas is the "Advent Joy Kit." This is simply a decorated box holding small wrapped gifts for each day during the month of December. The gifts should be inexpensive and useful: a comb, nail file, tape, note pads, little cheery notes or Scripture verses. Tailor the gifts to the person, of course. This spreads the joy of Advent through many long, lonely days for the elderly or shut-in.

Another idea for a gift that shows how much you value people and that doesn't cost money is the "coupon" gift. For children, coupons can entitle the bearer to one evening a week with Mom, a choice of activity for the whole family, an evening out with Mom and Dad, or fifteen minutes of uninterrupted conversation at bedtime.

Grandparents can give gifts of time to grandchildren: trips to the library, cooking lessons, a night at Grandpa's house once a month, and so on.

Here are more "different" ideas:

- hand down heirlooms or childhood keepsakes to children or grandchildren; one wise mother wrapped her heirloom dishes in identical boxes without designating the receiver, then let each of her three daughters choose a box
- a dinner invitation
- plants—take cuttings of favorite plants and root them before the holiday. To make inexpensive plant pots, punch holes in the bottom of coffee or tin cans, and decorate with self-stick paper, or yarn glued around the can
- give pretty glass jars of tea, hot chocolate mix, or other dry foods

But sometimes it's necessary to move beyond even these

124

homemade ideas for ways of valuing people. Perhaps a beginning point is to look for ways to give to people who are *really* in need. There are some substantial, year-long projects to consider if giving a Christmas basket to a needy family seems like only "token" charity.

Perhaps the family could start a savings box and then take a vote on Christmas Eve as to where the money will be given. Use the occasion to talk about the real meaning of Christmas, how people want to give gifts to Jesus, and how this is one way in which to do it.

Some year-around projects might work out better if you involve a group beyond your family, such as a group of interested persons at church. Is there a family who cares for a bedfast, disabled, or elderly person full time? Perhaps they'd appreciate being relieved on a regularly scheduled basis.

At our own church, concerns for people with special needs have spilled over into continuing projects like a "Clothes Closet" to make used clothing available free to needy persons, a soup kitchen, a community wide Big Brother-Big Sister program, a summer day camp for retarded youth and adults. We don't need to overwork ourselves at Christmas doing special "good deeds" when we're involved with others year around. This on-going emphasis on service to others also better represents Christ's approach: he didn't make good deeds a once-a-year shot.

Another way to help focus on Christ at Christmas is to make sure your activities include some worshipful or meditational times. Some families have a candle lighting ceremony on Christmas Eve. Some have held processions with lighted candles throughout the house, looking for a hidden "Christ child" that someone had placed beforehand. Others take lighted candles and join the flames together, the united flames symbolizing a rekindling of bonds of friendship, loyalty, and family. An old custom that comes from Ireland is burning a candle in the front window on Christmas Eve until it goes out on its own, and then going to bed.

We always had a mini "Christmas Eve program," fashioned similar to our Christmas program at church. But this program was not planned and staged by the adults. It was planned, directed, and carried out by us four children. We usually gave Mom and Dad "parts" in the program by assigning them poems or scriptures to read. So if you're feeling too harried to do everything you'd like to do at Christmas, remember that children like certain responsibilities and privileges delegated to them.

No family in which both parents spend a significant part of the week employed outside the home can manage to do everything they'd like for Christmas and still enjoy a restful, Christ-centered holiday. I'm finding that I value a relaxed and happy family much more than a perfectly clean house for the holidays. Candlelight will camouflage cobwebs, and joy on the face sparkles more than any spotless china! As I sit down in front of the manger scene to tell the story of Christ's birth to Michelle "just once more before bedtime," I realize that such experiences are infinitely more valuable than baking that extra batch of cookies. When one's focus is on Christ, it becomes easier to choose activities that nurture people. Ironically in the process, it often happens that we don't spend as much money as we would on a Madison Avenue-type Christmas!

18

Summertime:
Who Says the Living Is Easy?

A popular song from a few years ago began, "Summertime, an' the livin' is easy." And I often thought, of all the times it would be nice just to stay home, summer would be my pick. (Unless, of course, it would be an icy January morning when fighting snowsuits, mittens, and a slick road in an attempt to get to work on time is not worth the trouble.) I guess the truth is that mothers who stay home all the time might be glad to get out of the house during either of those times: in summer when the kids are underfoot all day and the list of "creative activities" has been absolutely exhausted, or in winter when everyone's cooped up by a bad storm. But summertime, for the mother who works outside the home, means doing gardening and canning or freezing at the end of an already exhausting day. And sometimes it means packing for a trip until midnight because you couldn't leave the office until five o'clock.

But while I say summertime isn't necessarily easy, the pace of living really is different in summer, whether we work out of the home or not. There are longer evenings and more outdoor activities—friendly chats across the fence with the

127

neighbors, leisurely picnics, puttering in flower beds and vegetable gardens. During the summer, formality loses out to informality and barefoot freedom. Even entertaining is more casual. We don't have to worry about cleaning the house for company—just have barbecues, use paper plates, and keep everyone outside!

But it still takes energy to successfully plan fun activities for the family that (1) don't blow the family budget, (2) can be done in the evenings, on weekends, or on days off, and (3) that don't shatter Mom and Dad's nerves. When it seems like it will take a major moving van to carry everything needed for a weekend camping trip with the kids, often it's easier and more relaxing just to stay home.

One way to save hassle and expense is to take one-day trips when the kids are young. That way some packing for overnight and some expense are eliminated. But I say it still takes a lot of effort and cooperation between husband and wife to make sure one partner doesn't end up doing most of the work.

Too often families awake to a nice Saturday wanting to do "something" but they can't think of any place to go. One way to solve this problem is to watch for ideas of places to go and things to do as you read newspapers and magazines. Clip these possibilities out all year long and keep them in a file. Then, when trying to decide on a family activity, dig out the file and look through it until something sounds inviting.

Another source for ideas is the local travel agency or chamber of commerce. Many of these associations publish brochures listing special summertime events—county fairs, apple blossom festivals, parades, outdoor concerts, guided tours of gardens or historical homes, art shows, and so on.

Or how about visiting the state or provincial capital? Many people live close enough to go sightseeing for a day. The capital city often has interesting places to visit like museums and zoos in addition to historical and government buildings.

Some families have made "searching for their roots" a family project. They visit old church or family cemeteries, courthouses, and distant relatives. You can make the project as simple or detailed as your family wants. Some facts may be found nearby, but others might require additional research and driving out of state. If this is the case, a family vacation could be planned around the search. Perhaps the hometown newspaper would even be interested in doing a feature story about the project.

Picnics are another traditional summertime activity, so why not try a breakfast picnic? It can be as elaborate as bacon, eggs, and pancakes sizzling over an open fire in the woods somewhere, or as simple as taking a bowl of granola, milk, and juice to a park. If your family is really energetic, go to a scenic location and watch the sunrise for a special treat. Only be sure and find out first what time the sun rises. I must have been about ten or eleven years old when I decided that I wanted to see the sunrise all by myself one spring morning. I got up when it was dark, and sat alone in our cold, damp orchard to await the sun. Well, I waited and waited, for what seemed like forever. Finally, I got so cold and discouraged that I gave up before I ever saw the sun!

Playing hide and seek with the kids is an old favorite that takes on a different dimension when played outdoors after dark. Smaller children may be just a bit scared, but adventurous types will enjoy the "thrill." I vividly remember playing "Seven Steps Around the House" with my cousins. We got so scared we always had to eat long stalks of celery to calm our nerves. (Instead of chewing fingernails, I guess.) If you choose to do this, just make sure everybody knows and understands the boundaries, so nobody gets lost!

Or simply take a walk on a clear night with children. Have everyone lie down on their backs and watch the stars. It's another whole wonderful world, one unequaled even by the special effects of wizards who create "Star Wars" spectacles.

Summer can be more than just a time for personal pleasure. Some of my best memories of summer are of days spent helping others. For several years in mid-May, my Dad took charge of organizing a work day when all the neighboring farmers brought their tractors, plows, and corn planters together and planted an entire farm in one day. The crops harvested in the fall went to an organization dedicated to feeding hungry people in the world. Kids helped out the best they could, doing errands and helping the moms put together a marvelous carry-in potluck lunch. Of course, if I'd have been a mom then, I'm not sure I'd have viewed it as such a fun day. It was hard work, glamorized in the first year by extensive media coverage—TV cameras and all. Now the hard work is forgotten, and only the terrific feeling of a community unified for one day remains.

But are such events only for farmers? How can we translate such projects for today's urban scene?

A friend of mine recently spearheaded a community project to build a creative playground for the town where she lives. She said that although the city and county are currently engaged in battle over an annexation issue, city and county residents together pitched in with manual labor, funds, and supplies to create a lovely, innovative play area for all the kids.

In another instance, a couple took their two-week vacation and volunteered to help in clean-up operations after a hurricane. Their regular jobs were sedentary, so this type of change-of-pace vacation restored them as much as lying around for two weeks at a beach would have.

But maybe just a one-day project sounds more manageable. Is there an older person living alone who can't afford help for a thorough housecleaning job? Organize a family— or two-family—project and make a day of it. Top the housecleaning off with a hot dog roast or fast food meal in the evening. Keep it simple, but have fun.

Many charitable organizations have fund-raising events in the summer. They often need people to do home baking, run concession stands, or help organize activities. One year my mother was kind of dreading her assignment to be in charge of demonstrating quilting for a small town's "sugar-maple festival." But she was surprised at the fun she had, answering tourists' questions about the art of quilting, showing eager hands how to quilt, and feeling pride when she realized the quilts displayed were worth hundreds of dollars to the sight-seers. She saw in a new way that she had a skill not everyone had.

Savor the little things of summer, too. One woman said she treasured the feel of her seven-year-old son's hand in hers as she walked along a beach shore, knowing that all too soon he wouldn't want to hold hands.[1]

Whatever our situation in life—if children are small, teen-agers, grown-up, whether we're single or married, working out or working at home—we can carve out experiences that rest and restore. Those words sound far-fetched on a busy day when I'm knee-deep freezing vegetables. But I know, too, the need to claim for myself the Bible verse, "Come unto me all you who are heavy laden, and I will give you rest." Restoration may come in unexpected places—in a quiet mo-ment alone with my spouse, in a spree of high hilarity playing a crazy game with the kids, or in a holy hush viewing a perfect evening sunset.

It's the little things that make summers, well, really *life,* memorable. Just think back to last summer, the year before, the year before that. What activities stand out most clearly? Then think back ten, fifteen, or twenty-five years, to child-hood. Sure, I remember the big things—the summer our family took a six-week trip out west, the summer I got to go camping at the beach, the summer I had my first crush, the summer I got married. But then there are also the little things—riding a bike on summer evenings after all the work was done, building a "club" house with my sisters and some neighbor kids and forming the "Miller Monkey Motel Club," shelling peas with Mom and playing "I'm Going On a Trip and I'm Gonna Take Along," planning parties, playing in the icy creek on a blistering day. More recently, I remember little things like the day my husband and I spontaneously took off on a drive to nowhere special and ended up sharing an impromptu picnic with groceries from a small country store and stopping for soft ice cream cones on the way home from town.

We don't necessarily have to plan big things to have an eventful summer. In fact, "big" things may be next to impossible given a pared down budget of time and money for such things. Let the little things happen and treasure them! I find it's easy to get so bogged down with the necessary things like canning and cleaning and going to work that I neglect the *needed* things like rest and spontaneity.

Even when there is just plain hard work to do, we can still have fun. Make games out of routine chores. Promise a treat for after lawn mowing. Make work a family project.

Wayne and Cathy raise strawberries each summer to sell. Their three young children help pick the strawberries. The money earned goes into a special family recreation kitty that they use for family outings. One year they used it for an all-day excursion to a large amusement park, where tickets are rather expensive for a whole family.

Parents soon learn that children want less-planned, less-structured family activities as they grow older.

My friend's mom did a "survey" of her children's interests, asking them what kinds of family activities they liked best. Mom was surprised. They wanted spontaneous rather than formally structured "family night" activities. They voted for outings that included other families. And, they said, don't try to "plan down" to the younger members of the family by "over-explaining" everything. They preferred having the younger ones ask questions if and when they didn't understand. This seemed to work and please everyone better.[2]

Finally, to store memories, some families keep a "Family Summer Memory Book." Collect small souvenirs like entrance tickets, paper napkins from restaurants, matchbooks, brochures, maps, postcards or photos. Date each entry and have various family members write down their memories. Pressed flowers or leaves can bring back smells and sights of a particular family outing. I think small children especially enjoy creating a family treasure book and leafing through it on cold winter nights.

The living may not be as easy as the song implies, but even amidst lots of hard work and late nights, summers can be fun and provide priceless learning times for everyone.

For example, the summer we took our sixteen-month-old daughter to the county fair for the very first time, I remember wondering beforehand whether the hassle would be worth it. We were sure to be up past her bedtime, there would be crowds, she might get fussy, and the stroller would be difficult to push over the bumpy fairgrounds. But I grew younger watching her delight and merriment as she sampled the strange texture of cotton candy; the thrill and look of "see how big I am" as she went round and round in the little play cars; the dazzle in her eyes as all three of us sat atop the Ferris wheel and viewed the lights, listened to the music and felt the excitement of the crowds; her quizzical look at seeing real live lambs and pigs and ducks and cows instead of pictures in a storybook.

Tired feet and changing diapers in the crowded restroom seem worth it now. Michelle may never remember her first county fair . . . but her mother and father will.

19

How Not to Get Depressed
When the Dusting Isn't Done

Most women are superstars at feeling guilty. I can go around laden with guilt all day if I want to.

If I sleep in ten extra minutes, I feel guilty for not being more disciplined. Then I rationalize my behavior by saying, "Well, I did stay up until 11:00 last night," but I chastise myself for having watched that silly old TV show anyway.

At breakfast I feel guilty for indulging in my cholesterol quota for this week by having two eggs with toast. At 7:30 A.M. Richard Simmons makes me feel guilty for not feeling like exercising, which reminds me that I forgot to let the dog out for his exercise last evening, too. By the time I get to my part-time job, I feel guilty that I had to leave Michelle at the babysitter's, that she's still on the bottle, and that I had to drive too fast to make it to work on time.

Of course I'm exaggerating, but not by much. We've probably all had days of wallowing in the sloughs of guilt, which is not very productive or wholesome.

Don't get me wrong. Guilt is an emotion given to us by God. It can be destructive and self-defeating, or it can alert us to responsibilities we've ignored or to things we might be trying to cover up.

The dictionary recognizes that there are at least two types of guilt. One is the guilt felt when a written law or moral code is violated. Another is guilt for imagined offenses. I think working mothers in particular suffer from guilt for imagined offenses. We're apt to think that any problem—from bed-wetting to thumbsucking—is a direct result of our working outside the home.

One counselor says that North American women especially are in the throes of a major guilt epidemic. Now that there are new opportunities and responsibilities for women, there are more ways to feel guilty when we can't do everything perfectly.[1]

Of course, women don't have a special corner on guilt. Men feel guilty, too, but for one reason or another they seem to handle it differently. Traditionally at least, women have felt their success in life was linked to their kids' success, whereas men tended to draw fulfillment from a job. In the same way, men have felt more guilt for job failures than for family setbacks. However, these differences between men and women are partly cultural and are probably changing as men have more involvement with their families and as women derive increasing fulfillment from paid jobs.

Some guilt is associated with unreal expectations, like feeling as though you must keep a house in picture-perfect order. Some guilt is the heavy kind, like blaming yourself for the breakup of a marriage. But whatever the nature of guilty feelings, they are usually trying to tell us something: that we're too perfectionistic, neurotic, or busy; or that we need to shape up spiritually.

The main point I'm making is this: if I'm feeling guilty, I should try to find the source. Whether it's about something insignificant like the dusting, or about something crucial like caring for elderly parents, I should own up to the guilt, examine it, and see if it's valid. Sometimes understanding the root of our guilty feelings can motivate us to do good things.

For example, if I decide it's ridiculous to worry about the dusting, then every time I begin to feel guilty about not dusting from that point on I can say, "That's ridiculous." If I decide it's important to worry about how Jill is doing in school, then I can take steps to find an acceptable solution to her math problems.

As parents, we sometimes dump unnecessary loads of guilt on ourselves by comparing kids. The new parents ask, "Why does our baby cry more than the Jones's? What are we doing wrong?" And the comparisons hardly stop with infancy. On through childhood, parents engage in a competitive game where there are no winners.

The first time I became acutely aware of this tendency was when I enrolled our thirteen-month-old in "Tots' Swim School." Inwardly, I gloated as Michelle happily did her "kicking" and "digging" while other tots seemed more interested in screaming. Then I felt inadequate when other toddlers advanced to "swimming" with floats long before Michelle was ready to try. There are only losers in this comparison game because the parents feel defeated, the child feels inadequate, and the other child and her parents are put at arms length by our comparisons.

So how do we work at reducing the myriad sources of guilt? One suggestion is to accept limitations. Who is capable of being a whiz on the job, a social butterfly, a perfect parent, and an artist all at the same time? Guilty feelings can help us decide on priorities.

Sometimes we just need to learn how to give a caring "no." Does being assertive and loving seem like an unworkable combination? Perhaps that's because our picture of assertive people has been flavored by unpleasant encounters of the assertive kind! We've met people who were obnoxiously aggressive or even violent who *claimed* they were "just being assertive." And we've all seen drivers on the highway who seemed more interested in driving assertively than defensively.

But we *can* learn to say "no" to requests and demands without feeling guilty, and without being unpleasantly aggressive. It won't happen overnight. It happens only by learning new patterns of responding, and by practicing those patterns over and over again until they become second nature.

To begin saying "no" without feeling guilty, try listing all the areas of life where assertiveness would be helpful or more satisfying. Try listening to see how often self-effacing statements creep into conversation. I've found that when I respond to others with assertive confidence in myself, people respond in a similar way, with respect. Oh, not always, but in general I've found this to be true.

It's the kind of wholeness Jesus demonstrated with his life. He treated the outcasts of society with the same respect and love he gave his friends. So the outcasts were elevated to a position of being "friends"—equals.

Assertiveness may include taking a firm look at the demands we put on ourselves as well. As working women, we can't always accomplish all that we'd like to. One of the keys to not getting depressed when the dusting isn't done is to become a realistic goal setter.

A goal is always something specific, something measurable. So one way to make sure I keep a goal is by establishing a clear-cut guide to measure my success by, like "repaint the living room *by Christmas*."

Now, I know of nothing more discouraging than comparing myself to a highly motivated superwoman who always assigns every job a priority, "A," "B," or "C," just like the experts say to do. I'm bothered by efficiency experts who measure every minute with "coffee spoons," and who seem

137

to place little value on spontaneity, creativity, and time for people. Not all satisfaction in life comes from crossing an item off a "Things-To-Do" list. Doing the unexpected, the unplanned—taking a quick course in ceramics just because I feel like it and it suits my schedule—is refreshing to a rigid goal setter.

But on the practical side, I know that spontaneity must be tempered with discipline. And that a laid-back approach to life must be balanced with realistic goals in order to accomplish what I really want in life.

Life is filled with so many interruptions, so many interesting, worthwhile things to do! Sometimes it's a matter of choosing between good and better things, of deciding between the *important* and the *urgent*. When my boss sends something to my desk marked urgent, I give it top priority. Too often I fail to do that when assigning priorities to my personal activities. But with a list nearby, I can quickly decide between going to that home-sale party and spending time with my kids. One is on my list of priorities, the other is not.

For most of us the problem isn't setting goals, but accomplishing them. We begin the new year with a whole list of new year resolutions that we soon push to the back of a drawer for the rest of the year. How do we keep time from leaking away in unplanned TV watching, idle yakking, or busy work?

One way is to "go public" with your goals. One year I kept my list of goals right inside my cupboard door where I store plates, cups, and glasses. It's a place where I can see the goals frequently, but it's not quite as public and open to view as it would be if I posted them on the bulletin board! After all, some of my goals are rather private.

My really close friends and relatives—the ones who help wash dishes—are interested in my list of goals. One day my sister asked, "Well, how are you doing on your goals for the year?" It was time for honest confession! "Well, I am pretty good at spending free time with my daughter and at writing for at least two hours a week. I did pretty well on the exercise goal for awhile—and I'm really trying hard on the stop nagging one. But I really have failed to spend more time reading the Bible and in prayer." Publicly stating your goals can make you more accountable for achieving them as friends and relatives remind you to examine your progress.

Another way to keep the seconds from frittering away is to use even the smallest bits and pieces of time wisely.

Most writers' idea of "Fantasy Island" would be a year locked away on Key West writing the "Great American Novel." When I realized I would never be so lucky as to be awarded such a fantasy, I started looking around for any free time I did have available. Tucked away between housekeeping, working, raising kids, and spending time with a husband were *minutes*. Not whole years or even weeks, or hours, but ten minutes here, thirty minutes there. Well, I began trying to grab those minutes and devote them to fulfilling my dream of being a part-time writer. Almost anything is possible if you set realistic goals and stick to them!

Sometimes one goal interferes, or seems to interfere, with another. Say that one of my goals is spending at least one half hour of play and attention with each child every day. Maybe another goal is being available to neighbors when they need help. Most likely, my neighbor needs help babysitting just when I had finally planned to sit down and read to my daughter. It is times like this when it helps to remain flexible. I must remind myself that I needn't be frustrated when the time set aside for one thing gets gobbled up because I want to listen to my sister's problems for a half hour on the phone.

It's usually not the good things that rob us of goal achievement, but plain old procrastination or laziness. "I'll just sit down and watch this half hour of my favorite talk show before I get started on the wash," I say. But by the time the talk show is over, Michelle has dumped her toys all over the living room and fed the cat all over the kitchen. I help her clean up the mess and a salesman comes to the door. By the time I think about the laundry again, it's only a half hour before I need to leave for a doctor's appointment and there's no time to sort clothes for the wash.

I probably don't have to recite the gory details of mornings like that. Whether it's at the office, at the schoolroom, or at home, we all know how procrastination eats away at the time we value. One good bit of advice I've heard is: "Do it. Do it now. Do it right." While that may seem simplistic, it can be good motivation when I really don't feel like doing anything.

Reaching goals takes hard work. There is nothing magical about writing objectives down on a piece of paper and then sitting back and waiting for them to work.

We can bum along through life, getting by with a minimum of effort and letting others tackle the really big challenges. But to me, that's not really the kind of person Christ asks us to be. He gave his best and asks us to do the same. That does not mean being a superwoman. In fact, it may mean letting the dusting go in favor of writing a letter to Grandma or inviting a friend in for tea. It may mean saying no to sitting on a committee in order to gain one night at home with the family, or to work on that master's degree.

We keep growing by setting worthy but attainable goals—high enough to challenge, but within grasp if God wills and if we're willing to do the work.

20

How a Calico Cat Preached a Sermon

It was the time in the church service that is open for anyone to share prayer concerns, praise items, and personal events. Five-year-old Heather's eyes reflected both her seriousness and joy as she proudly announced to the congregation that her family had gotten brother and sister kittens that week. She had named the girl kitten Patches because of its calico coat. Buttons was a boy and was called that because he had two white splotches on his black tummy.

I imagine that everyone thought, "How cute. She actually thinks kittens are important enough to mention at church." But there was a lesson there, too. So often we adults are too shy, embarrassed, or reluctant to share the small events from our lives, for fear others will think our concerns are not significant enough to bother them with.

Heather trusted our little congregation. She believed that we would respect her feelings of joy over the addition of kittens to her life. What she did was more than just "cute." Heather and her kittens had preached the only sermon I remember from worship that day. Children have delightful ways of ministering to needs we didn't even know we had.

141

Someone has said that older mothers (those of us who had our first child after age twenty-eight) sometimes act as if we *invented* motherhood. We're so enthralled by pregnancy, childbirth, nursing, the first tooth—in short, childhood—that we tend to forget that such wonderful things have been going on for centuries.

I'm aware that some people don't care too much for children. And certainly it's possible to put children on a pedestal, to idolize them. It's also possible to bore friends and co-workers to death with endless tales of my little darling's latest adventures. But I'm also aware that kids can teach us many lessons of love and life when we're tuned into that possibility.

Of course, other adults teach us too, all the time. But sometimes we adults are too inhibited by proper etiquette or by our doubts, fears, and need for acceptance to respond naturally like a child does.

We can learn from watching children to more freely express our emotions. A one-year-old is not ashamed to let the tears pour forth when Mother goes "bye-bye." And the tears quickly change to laughter as the babysitter wisely turns the child's attention to a favorite toy. Adults, on the other hand, may be a little bit embarrassed by the tears which appear when we say goodbye to friends or family moving away.

As adults we may try to disguise our need for love and affection. Children seek affection without any embarrassment. At twenty months, Michelle often pleaded "hold you." She didn't have her grammar right, but her message was crystal clear. Are we as free to tell a friend or spouse, "I need to be held. Will you hug me?"

In a book called *The Ministry of the Child*, Dennis Benson and Stan Stewart go so far as to say adults need the care of children if they are to grow.[1] And they're not just talking about parents. Most of us, whether we have children of our own or not, are touched daily by children. They may be children of friends or relatives, or children we meet casually in the supermarket.

Again, I'm not advocating that everyone has to be wild about all children. Children also get on one's nerves and push one to the point of exasperation. Children fight with each other and can be unbelievably cruel. But since we were each a child, I think it's important to be in touch with our own childlike qualities that can make life more uninhibited, loving, and giving.

When our daughter was just learning to walk, of course she had lots of falls. But one day she managed to cut her lip, her gums, and a big bruise appeared by the side of her eye.

For the rest of the day I "babied" Michelle. I thought about how sore I would have been if I'd taken a fall like that. As I rocked her to sleep at bedtime, I felt such an incredible closeness! Michelle looked like she felt it too—peaceful and contented. The kitchen was full of dishes, the living room was full of toys, and the dryer was loaded with clothes to be folded, but all that could wait.

I wouldn't want to "baby" her like that every day, because I wouldn't want her to begin to expect it. I like for her to be content spending time by herself, too. But for that day I felt a little more in touch with my own vulnerability to the knocks and hurts of life, and my own needs to be comforted.

Another example of how children lead adults can be observed in the reactions of older people. They especially seem to love the healing touch of small children.

One day we were visiting in a nursing home. Michelle began to get a little restless, so I took her for a walk down the hall. At one nurses' station the elderly residents were gathered, and several motioned for us to stop and talk. Michelle was wide-eyed with curiosity as she watched all the women beckoning to her, trying to catch her attention or win her smile.

Another woman, hearing the noise, emerged from her room. Michelle held out her hand and the woman took it and held it momentarily. One of the other women confided, "That's Bessie. Never says a thing. That's somethin' to get anything out of *her*." Bessie followed us to the door of the nursing home as we left later on. She never said a thing, just stared.

A small child can draw out a response from someone who has lost most other contact with the world. Michelle did it in complete innocence, of course, not knowing that of all the women in that circle, the silent one was the one who most needed some sign of affection or recognition.

It's easy to see how nursing home residents need the touch and wonderful presence of small children in their lives; but Michelle needed that old woman's touch just as well . . . to see that people come in all ages.

Middle-aged people and young marrieds also need reminders from children. Bill's boss asked him to take on a moonlighting project. For extra pay, he'd only have to work three nights a week for a month.

"Well, we could certainly use the money," Connie said. "And I'm glad your boss respects your work enough to consider you for the job. But your son needs you evenings. I need you. Probably *more* than we need the money."

"I know," Bill sighed uncomfortably. "What's more, I need my son, and you too. Maybe there's a way we can spread the work out over four months and I'd only have to be gone one evening a week."

Too many times we focus only on the fact that our children need us, but the fact is, *we* need our children, too. We need their gentle ways of making us stop and see priorities through youngish eyes.

I'm reminded of the time parents brought their little children to Jesus to receive a blessing. Jesus' friends felt he was too busy to be bothered by these parents and children and tried to turn them away. But Jesus invited the children onto his lap and said, "Let the children come to me . . . for the kingdom of heaven belongs to such as these."[2] At another time he said, "Unless you become like a little child, you cannot enter the kingdom of heaven."[3] These words simply mean that the generous, loving, sacrificial nature of little children is an essential part of Christian life.

Occasionally we meet adults who have not lost childlike qualities through the years. They still have some of the gentleness, spontaneity, and openness of a small child. They can cast aside their dignity and stuffiness and play a silly game of "horsey" on the floor. They take the time to enjoy long walks through parks and smell abundant June roses. They can let loose and enjoy a good belly laugh when the occasion calls for it. I've frequently said that I find myself laughing with our child like I haven't laughed since I was a little girl myself.

A proverb says, "A merry heart does us good, like medicine." When children help us smile and laugh, they are giving us a healthy shot of "feel-good" medicine.

Gerry especially has not lost those childlike qualities. He is a serious graduate student, a whiz on college entrance exams and things like that. But if given the chance, he'll get so wrapped up in a conversation with a friend who is hurting that deadlines for major papers are temporarily forgotten. At three years of age, his oldest son had an extraordinary gift for language use and storytelling. I think it was partly due to his parents' ability to stop and listen intently to their son without putting him off.

Often we're too busy to notice the caring qualities our children exhibit. But taking the time to do so and then to tell the child about it is very important, for their growth and ours! Say something like, "You showed you are very grown up when you helped Tommy fix his bike, especially when I know you wanted to go fishing." Try to be completely natural in making such comments, because children quickly sense a

145

patronizing attitude. Remember also to give the praise in private, especially if the child is older, so he isn't embarrassed.

Too often we, as parents, feel our children are a bother to other people. I had to remember that when a friend offered to hold Michelle when she was only an infant. The friend wasn't just doing something for me and the baby; she was satisfying a very real need in herself. Often I am too shy about taking friends up on their offers to help, feeling they can't really mean it and not wanting to impose.

To summarize, celebrate children with all their gifts! Celebrate older people who bring out the small gifts of children! Celebrate those who may not have children of their own, but who provide relief for those burdened with the responsibilities of parenting! And be glad for any creative, childlike generosity present in ourselves and others!

21

How to Live
Happily Ever After (More or Less)

While pushing Michelle's stroller through our local mall, I noticed, out of the corner of my eye, a man approaching me. Was he going to grab my purse? Mug me in broad mall light? No. He simply said, "Ma'am, I think you're losing your coat belt." Indeed, I was. It had slipped out of its loop and was snaking my leg like a silly monkey tail.

He had the grace not to point out what else I was losing. Anybody that goes alone to a mall with a toddler deserves a medal for combat bravery. With Pampers overflowing from the diaper bag, Michelle dropping cracker crumbs in stores that said "No food," and a package slipping from my grasp, I must have looked like the proverbial harried housewife. I wasn't quite a curlers-and-bathrobe case, but I definitely qualified as "slightly frumpled."

I hitched up my coat belt, flashed him a grateful grin, and envied the sleek young salesgirl slithering off to her coffee break. Her makeup was definitely Cover Girl, perfume by Prince Machabelli, outfit by Oscar de la Renta (or at least a small town copy), and hair like she had just stepped out of a Paris salon.

147

Is there life after motherhood? Is it possible to live happily ever after? Will Humpty Dumpty ever get "put back together" again?

Motherhood is more difficult than I ever imagined. But like most mothers say, it is also more fulfilling than I ever imagined. It's hard to make the mental transition from child to parent. Sometimes I pinch myself—*I'm a mother now just like I remember my mother when I was little. Will my kids enjoy their childhood like I did?*

What does it take to have a happy family? A family may get along well and have good times together, but not be able to explain, spontaneously, how to create such a happy family. Or a family may quarrel and bicker all the time, and not have a clue as to why they're unhappy. Oh, they may have ideas about who is to blame, but they don't know the *real* reasons.

No family is perfect. That seems so obvious, yet there are a number of people who needlessly frustrate themselves by expecting the impossible out of fellow family members.

Patience is the key word here, and patience implies hard emotional work. Patience is something that really does not develop unless one has experienced circumstances that are less than ideal, where potentially there *could* have been a burst of impatience or anger. Patience helps to maintain a happy family atmosphere.

I can almost see my husband snickering. "Practice what you preach," he'll say when he reads this, and he'll be right. Although other people see me as an easygoing, patient type, he knows how suddenly I can explode in a childish tantrum. It's then that I thank God that my husband seems to have the patience needed to maintain control and get things back on an even keel.

Since people are not perfect, it takes patience and maturity to live with others, especially in a unit as close as the family. As it is stated in Romans 5:3–4 (NIV), ". . . We also rejoice in our sufferings, because we know that suffering produces

148

perseverance; perseverance, character; and character, hope."

These principles apply to extended families, families without children, families without one of the parents, single-people-families as they relate to roommates and friends, and families who choose to live together in community.

Happiness or unhappiness in a family often depends on *how* situations are faced. Is there a healthy sense of humor amidst the daily irritations? Healing laughter can be the lubricant that helps a family function without squeaks and breakdowns. Children pick up this positive atmosphere and attitude very quickly, just as they pick up a negative, pessimistic approach to life.

I know of some families that have parents who complain about everything from high taxes to bad government to how rotten Mr. So-and-So is. "The world is unfair and I'm out to get all I can before I collapse from a heart attack."

Well, these may be the facts of life, but if negativism is what children hear, it is the attitude toward life they will probably develop. And that pessimism, like a black cloud hanging over the household, will be the daily atmosphere.

I'm not suggesting that children should be sheltered from the unpleasant and unjust sides of life and society. An honest approach is still usually the most healthy. The family is the best breeding ground for respect for other people and their opinions, whether or not we agree with their philosophy or actions.

Alice shared how her children were harassed on the school bus by bigger children who hit her children's heads with books, pulled their hair, and in general teased and mocked them. There didn't seem to be much Alice and her husband could do to stop the situation, so instead they faced it honestly.

They let their children know that they sympathized with them and their feelings and that it was okay to feel angry.

Then they asked the children for some ideas of what they could do to put an end to the harassment. The whole family brainstormed for awhile, and at the end of the session the children commented that they at least felt better, even though the problem wasn't solved. Their feelings had been recognized. Their attitude toward the other children began to change. I'm sure this experience helped Alice's children mature in their attitudes toward others and helped them grow together as a happy family.

Kids will also quickly pick up a parent's attitude about having children. I know of a mother who frequently told her two-year-old, "Oh, Monica . . . you're terrible," after Monica had spilled her cereal, written on the walls, or misbehaved in some other way. Monica soon picked this up and returned, "Oh Mommy, you're terrible."

On the other hand, children can also sense satisfaction and joy, which directs the whole spirit of family life.

As I've already indicated, I grew up on a farm. I remember my childhood as being extremely happy—almost unrealistically so. Yet we *worked hard*: baling hay in the summertime (and then having a watermelon party afterwards), harvesting the garden produce (and making games out of it), working from 10:00 P.M. to 2:00 A.M. catching and carrying heavy chickens to a truck to be sold (and then celebrating with a late ice cream party). My parents weren't disobeying child labor laws. Chickens have to be caught at night when it's dark so they can't see to get away! I'm not praising the "good old days" or idolizing farm life, but rather wish to show that mixing work and fun can apply to present society also.

An urban family can enjoy all the art and theater and libraries that cities offer. Or a family project of cleaning the apartment or washing the car can be followed by a picnic in the park.

The external influences on family life may have changed, but the internal workings remain the same. If the family base

150

is not a happy, cooperating unit, then no amount of activity will make it fun. When traveling through suburb, town, or countryside, I often try to imagine whether the families inside pretty houses are happy or sad, fighting or laughing. An expensive or elaborate vacation trip will be miserable if family members are at odds with one another. A trip to a million-dollar resort or amusement park will not make a happy family. But things like love and patience and acceptance will.

What can be done on a *daily* basis to create a happy, pleasant home life?

Mealtime is an important element in creating the overall tone of a household. In fact, just having mealtime *together* is a major accomplishment when there are four or five schedules to mesh. I know some families in which the kids literally don't know what sitting down to a table and eating together is. For many modern families, most "meals" are eaten on the run between work, school, TV, and extracurriculars. But even with your hectic schedules try to plan at least several meals together a week. When sitting together at the table, have each family member share the most interesting thing that happened to him or her during the day. Exchange humorous incidents, jokes, or ask riddles.

Another way to foster a good home life is to set aside some time each day to read together. Young children love to have stories read aloud to them. And reading develops creative thinking much more than TV does.

Or have a place where you can chart a child's growth on a wall. One family says that even after the children were grown they enjoyed looking at the marks and reminiscing about times when they were younger.

Teach children about gardening and make it fun! Let them have a little plot of their own that they can plant, weed, water, and care for. Even in the city seeds can be sprouted in little boxes, or larger plants can be grown in bushel baskets. Children will enjoy the rewards of their efforts.

I think another reason my childhood was so happy was that my parents' love for each other was very obvious. They were naturally affectionate and didn't mind showing their fondness for each other in front of us children. In fact, we joke about the fact that Dad has "ruined" so many family photos by stealing a big kiss just as the camera shutter was snapped, that the photo album ought to be R-rated.

Although I got embarrassed sometimes when I was a kid at the kissing and hugging, inside I felt comforted and secure. Their actions in all other areas of life were in harmony with their honest demonstration of affection.

One of the best things a family can do together may be to reach out to others. Broaden family concerns to include the needs of others.

I especially remember a steady stream of visitors from other countries in our home. For many years we hosted an international student at Christmas. They cooked special, strange-tasting dishes for us, we took them on real old-fashioned sleigh rides, and invariably I'd develop an adolescent crush on one of the fellows. I've forgotten some of the countries and most of the names, but what has stuck with me is that people the world over are the same inside, regardless of color, religion, or language.

There are many other ways to share as a family and bring happiness into your lives. One family bakes cookies with another family, and together they deliver the cookies to shut-ins and older people they know. This doesn't have to be just at Christmas, but any time!

Especially keep single-parent families in mind when planning activities. Invite them over to share a picnic or go on an outing.

The happiest times in families come when we unselfishly share what we have with others. When money is scarce and time is limited, sometimes it takes quite a bit of creativity to come up with sharing activities that don't empty the bank or energy account.

My young family isn't far enough along to provide me with scores of illustrations on "family activities." So permit me one more story from my growing up days, which we kids all remember as one of the "best" family times ever.

It was a Christmas when money was especially tight. In fact, Mom and Dad had threatened that there might not be any "Christmas" for us—no gifts. We were not to expect more than one small present from them.

In other years we had enjoyed sharing from our bounty with a needy family in the community. We usually asked for a name from the Salvation Army or from welfare and felt like Santa Claus buying gifts for Girl, age 7; Boy, age 2; Baby, age 6 months. We also bought several boxes of groceries and a ham to take to the family on Christmas Eve. Somehow, it never felt like Christmas until we had shared with another family.

Well, that memorable Christmas when we went around feeling sorry for ourselves because there wasn't going to be much, Mom announced that she didn't think we'd even be able to afford to continue our tradition of getting a family's name from the Salvation Army.

Christmas Eve came and we went caroling with the church folks to some neighboring homes where Christmas appeared to be even slimmer than ours. In one home especially, I remembered six pairs of little eyes watching us with uncomfortably keen stares as we tried to sing "Joy to the World." The father talked about how there weren't any presents, or much food, nor even any shoes to wear to the church service we had invited them to attend. It wasn't easy to go to sleep that Christmas Eve.

Then Christmas morning came and suddenly the stack of presents beneath our own tree seemed mountainous after all. Between what people had given to us, and what we kids had bought for each other, it didn't look nearly as bleak as we had feared. We all sat around with sober faces though—one family on our minds.

I don't remember who thought of it first, but unexpectedly we found ourselves rushing around to find some of our best, now outgrown toys to wrap. Mom and Dad scoured the pantry and bulging freezer for home-frozen roasts, steaks, and hamburger. That Christmas morning, before we even got around to opening our own presents (something unheard of), we all voted to visit the Bennett family with the baskets we had pulled together.

People might say we were just soothing our own consciences, satisfying our own need to be able to help someone else. All I know is that I'll never forget the pure joy and surprise and delight in those six little pairs of eyes as they tore recklessly into the boxes we had brought. And our relationship with that particular family didn't stop there. It has continued in different forms through the years, all year long.

God provided the supreme example of love with recklessness of another kind—of giving up his Son to death so that we might know eternal life. As a mother, I can now begin to understand his gift in a way I didn't before.

There is life after motherhood—a life fuller, wearier, and "worrieder" than before. There is happiness in varying doses, although it may not be the fairytale kind of happiness, nor even the "ideal Christian family" variety. There are hurts, grief, depression, and fatigue.

But with God "putting me together," I have hopes for making it. I'm not talking about a superficial, tacky, "God-has-all-the-answers" kind of together. I'm talking about a faith that recognizes failures and heartaches, yet brings wholeness into a life pulled in many directions: job, children, spouse, church, community, and time for me. The knowledge of how often God has sustained me in the past is what gives me confidence to keep trying, even when life gets slightly frumpled.

Notes

CHAPTER 1:

1. Alice Lake, "Three for the Seesaw: How a First Baby Changes a Marriage." *Redbook* (April 1974): 99.
2. Elisabeth Keiffer, "What Happens to Marriage When a Wife Goes Back to Work?" *Good Housekeeping* (September 1975): 101.
3. Lake, "Three for the Seesaw," 152.

CHAPTER 2:

1. "Is Parenting a Right or a Privilege to Be Earned?" *Family Life* 37 n. 5 (September–October 1977): 1.
2. Marvin Grosswirth, "Kids, Who Needs 'Em?" *Scientific Digest* (October 1976): 72.
3. "How Do You Really Feel About Having Children?" *Redbook* (September 1977): 117.
4. Malcolm Muggeridge, "From Fantasy to Reality," *Christianity Today* (21 April 1978): 11.
5. Nancy and Chip McGrath, "Why a Baby?" *New York Times Magazine* (25 May 1975): 27.
6. *Ibid.*, 10.

CHAPTER 3:

1. Gina Bari Kolata, "Early Warnings and Latest Cures for Infertility." *Ms.* (May 1979): 35.

2. Eileen Williams Theim, "Why Can't I Have a Baby?" *Ladies' Home Journal* (October 1979): 22.
3. Deidre Laiken, "The Best Way to Deal With Infertility." *Self* (December 1979): 93.

CHAPTER 5:

1. Wendy Haskell Meyer, "A Special Delivery." *The National Observer* (12 October 1974): 26.

CHAPTER 6:

1. T. Berry Brazelton, M.D., *Doctor and Child* (New York: Delacorte Press, 1970), xviii, xix.
2. Mardel Asbury Crandall, "A Young Mother's Story." *Redbook* (October 1981): 180.
3. Brazelton, *Doctor and Child,* 70.
4. *Ibid.,* 71.
5. *Ibid.,* 66.

CHAPTER 7:

1. Contents of this chapter reprinted from *Christian Living,* "Should I Go Back to Work or Not?" Melodie Davis, August 1980, pp. 20–23.

CHAPTER 8:

1. Kris Miller Tomasik, "The Great American Balancing Act." *Today's Christian Woman* (Fall 1980): 100.
2. Letty Cottin Pogrebin, "How Do Children Really Feel When Their Mothers Work?" *Ladies' Home Journal* (October 1979): 68.
3. *Ibid.,* 237.
4. Tomasik, "Balancing Act," 99.
5. Questions are based on "Parents Checklist." *The Washington Post* (19 August 1981): C–6.

CHAPTER 10:

1. Bernice Weissbourd, "Declarations of Dependence." *Parents* (January 1983): 70.
2. *Ibid.*
3. Dr. Ross Campbell, *How to Really Love Your Child* (Fullerton, CA: Victor Books, 1980), 109.

CHAPTER 11:

1. Alta Mae Erb, Interview on "Your Time" radio program (April 1979). Produced by Margaret Foth for the Mennonite Church.
2. James L. Hymes, Jr., *The Child Under Six* (New Jersey: Prentice Hall, 1961), 172–174.
3. Erb, "Your Time."

CHAPTER 12:

1. Contents of this chapter reprinted from *Christian Living*, "Get Us to the Church on Time." Melodie Davis, August 1982, pp. 8–11.

CHAPTER 13:

1. Joy Wilt, *Surviving Fights with Your Brothers and Sisters* (Waco, TX: Word, Inc., 1978), 23.
2. *Ibid.*, 34.
3. *Ibid.*, 88.
4. Carole and Andrew Calladine, "Raising Siblings." *Family Circle* (28 August 1979): 130.
5. *Ibid.*
6. *Ibid.*

CHAPTER 14:

1. Nancy Lewis, "The Needle Is Like an Animal." *Children Today* (January/February 1978): 18–21.
2. Audrey T. McCollum, "The Special Stress That Can Break—Or Make—A Marriage." *Parents* (April 1976): 68.
3. *Ibid.*, 35.

CHAPTER 15:

1. Daniel J. Safer and Richard P. Allen, *Hyperactive Children* (Baltimore, MD: University Park Press, 1976), ix.
2. Kenneth Heiting, *When Your Child Is Hyperactive* (St. Meinrad, IN: Abbey Press, 1978), 75.
3. *Ibid.*, 48.
4. Sheila Cragg, *Tantrums, Toads, and Teddy Bears* (Scottdale, PA: Herald Press, 1979), preface.
5. *Ibid.*, 196.

CHAPTER 16:

1. *TV Mini-file*, A. C. Nielsen report, (New York: Television Information Office, 1982).
2. "TV or not TV?" *Mennonite Brethren Herald* (12 November 1976): 32.
3. *Television Awareness Training Leader's Manual* (New York: Media Action Research Center, Inc., 1977), 3:3.
4. *Ibid.*, 70.
5. Matthew 6:25–34, paraphrased.

CHAPTER 18:

1. Ruth E. Johnson, "God Gave Me A Summer." *Family Life Today* (August 1978): 3.
2. Helen Good Brenneman, *The House by the Side of the Road* (Scottdale, PA: Herald Press, 1971), 113.

CHAPTER 19:

1. Wendy Davis, "Guilt: Modern Woman's Old-Fashioned Burden." *Ladies' Home Journal* (July 1981): 26.

CHAPTER 20:

1. Dennis Benson and Stan J. Stewart, *The Ministry of the Child* (Nashville: Abingdon Press, 1978), 11.
2. Matthew 19:14 (NIV).
3. Mark 10:15, paraphrased.